STANDING OVATIONS

STANDING OVATIONS

And Other Memories of

a Texas Baby Boomer

TERRY L. BROXSON

iUniverse, Inc.
New York Lincoln Shanghai

STANDING OVATIONS
And Other Memories of a Texas Baby Boomer

iUniverse books may be ordered through booksellers or by contacting:

iUniverse
2021 Pine Lake Road, Suite 100
Lincoln, NE 68512
www.iuniverse.com
1-800-Authors (1-800-288-4677)

ISBN-13: 978-0-595-42146-6 (pbk)
ISBN-13: 978-0-595-86485-0 (cloth)
ISBN-13: 978-0-595-86484-3 (ebk)
ISBN-10: 0-595-42146-6 (pbk)
ISBN-10: 0-595-86485-6 (cloth)
ISBN-10: 0-595-86484-8 (ebk)

Printed in the United States of America

THE GOLDEN YEARS

Here I am at the Golden Age,
And since I have become a sage,
I feel that I should write it down—
With awesome words—most profound
To tell of deeds—by my own hand
So generations may understand,
(or with frustration—scratch their head,
And wonder what it was I said!)

They call these the "Twilight Years",
So far away from boos and cheers.
Experience and knowledge I have galore,
But no one listens any more!
"How is your dad?" someone will say.
My son will answer, "He passed away."

So here is to The Golden Years,
A time of peace—too late for tears,
But still—as far as I can see,
It ain't what it's cracked up to be!

By: Gil Broxson (1986)

Contents

IRENE

On a 100 degree day in August Zoe and I are driving through East Texas headed to Beaumont to attend a funeral service for Zoe's eighty-seven year old Aunt Irene. Zoe and I have been married over thirty years, so I knew Irene pretty well. She had been a widow for about as long as we had been married, and, frankly, I thought of her as a mean, nasty old woman who ragged on anyone around her. Now let me make it clear. I was not the only one in the family who thought this.

She didn't have two nickels to rub together. She had her house rebuilt as a community service project of Home Depot. She wondered and asked, "Why me? I am nothing special." She must have had a sweet side I didn't know. Zoe said she was great to her when she was a kid. I thought the funeral would be small with too much preaching.

Apparently, when her husband died, she decided to get involved with the Beaumont Community Theater. She couldn't act, was a bad dancer, a horrible singer ... but this little old rotund lady showed up at every audition. Most of their plays were musicals, so she had to sing at the audition. She always sang "Good Night Irene" in a high squeaky voice. It was so bad that those at the audition started singing along with her just to cover up the noise, but she always got a part in the chorus, and always in the back. If it was a non-musical, she got a part in the crowd scenes—maybe a line every now and then—and so it went for thirty years—audition, rehearsals, performance, cast party—this pushy little broad forcing her way onto the stage.

At the same time she became a volunteer with the Chamber of Commerce. It was said at the funeral by the president of the Chamber that for many years she attended every ribbon cutting in the City of Beaumont as an ambassador for the city—big new buildings ribbon cutting or tattoo parlor ribbon cutting—if a photo was taken she was in the front, and if food was served she was in the front too, thus forcing herself again onto the stage of life.

Now the funeral—there was a little preaching as she was also a longtime member of the Methodist church. Then the Chamber of Commerce president got up and told his stories of Irene, and the director of the Community Theater telling his stories and ending the funeral with 200-plus people on their feet singing:

"Irene, goodnight, Irene, goodnight,

Goodnight, Irene, goodnight, Irene,

I'll see you in my dreams.

Sometimes I live in the country,

Sometimes I live in town,

Sometimes I have a great notion;

To jump in the river and drown.

Irene, goodnight, Irene, goodnight

Goodnight, Irene, goodnight Irene,

I'll see you in my dreams."

And giving her the standing ovation she always craved and so richly earned.

After being there and seeing this, it occurs to me that we ought to change how funerals end. Each one I had been to up to this point ended with a prayer, but for a life well lived; we should be giving the person ... a standing ovation.

THE BAPTIST CHURCH

I grew up in Midland, Texas, having moved there with my family when I was two years old in 1948. Life in West Texas is marked by heat, sand, wind and more sand. My dad used to say he could sit on the back porch and see tomorrow coming two days off.

My kid brother and I had one other constant in our lives, the Baptist church. Our church was organized in 1948, probably because I moved to Midland. It is still a very vibrant church—despite the fact that I have not been there in years.

From my earliest recollection, if the doors of the church were open, we were there … Sunday School, Sunday morning services, Training Union, Sunday evening services, Wednesday services, the Royal Ambassadors, Lottie Moon special offering week, foreign missions, vacation bible school, youth-led revivals … on and on and on.

In the late fifties and early sixties there were some distractions. For example, on Saturday mornings I would go bowling at Shamrock Lanes in the youth programs. The old joke was that it got the kids out of the streets and into the alleys. More to the point it got us out of the house. On Saturday afternoons around 4PM on Channel 7, KOSA TV, a local rock and roll band would perform. Every week this kid (a little older than me) would start the program with his theme song "Ooby Dooby." In fact, in our house we called him Ooby Dooby. "Hey, Mom it's time for Mr. Ooby Dooby."

I got two kinds of education growing up. There was the kind they taught at the Baptist church and the kind they taught at Midland Independent School District. On most occasions this was not a problem—but some times—well, like my buddies on the high school debate team, Jimmy and Bryce. Jimmy was a Presbyterian and as far as

I knew we Baptists didn't have any reason why he would not go to Heaven. Of course he would have to wait for us Baptists to get in first.

Bryce was another matter—you see he was Catholic—and well they drank beer and wine, and gambled, and prayed to idols. I didn't think there was any way he would get into Heaven, but Bryce made better grades than I did, so I was not about to debate with him. Then, there was the small issue of my father. You see he liked to drink beer and wine, and gamble, but I never saw or heard of him praying to an idol. But then, I didn't see him in the Baptist church either.

And there was the space race, must have been in '61 or '62. One Sunday morning the Sunday school teacher, Colonel Mize, made the sobering observation, "You know I don't think God likes us messing around up there in his heaven." Lordy, I had visions of those satellites getting blasted out of orbit. Well, didn't happen, not yet anyway.

There were other educational opportunities on Sunday night after Training Union and evening services—they involved members of the opposite sex. Fact of the matter is it was how and where I learned to kiss girls. This is how it worked … three or four guys and three or four girls would jump in a car (cars were bigger in those days) and we'd drive around listening to "Run Around Sue" and "Tell Laura I Love Her" on the radio. We'd be on the sharp lookout for cars with one tail light or one head light. The first person to see one would yell out "PUDUNKEL" (one head light) or "PUDIDDLE" (one tail light). If you were the first guy to call out you got to kiss the girl of your choice. But this was equal opportunity—a girl calling out first got to kiss the boy of her choice. When I was in high school Sunday evening services were well attended by the youth of our church, and you would be amazed at how many cars in Midland had only one tail light or one head light.

An unexpected thing happened in 1964—I graduated from high school—not knowing what to do with my life I decided to go to college, a good small college—a Baptist college—not too far, but far enough. Hardin Simmons University in Abilene, Texas decided that they would accept my father's money and make a place for me. In September 1964 I escaped from the Baptist church in my home town. Dang, I was a new man.

But, I had not escaped the Baptist church. At Hardin Simmons life in the dorm was not bad. During my freshman year I did not have a car, but the campus had a cafeteria and your meal ticket gave you twenty meals a week, but not twenty one. On Sunday night the cafeteria was closed, so the only option to eat was to go to one of the Baptist churches where they served "free" Sunday night dinner "to students attending Training Union."

Well, with no car I walked across the street to the Baptist Church—me and all the other freshman with no cars. There we dined on tuna fish sandwiches made with sweet pickles and a side of potato salad—and of course with no cars there was no Pudunkel or Pididdle.

In October 1964, my life changed. I met Burl Bumpus, a senior, with a car and saw an ad in the newspaper: "LAVENDERS CAFETERIA … ALL YOU CAN EAT … SUNDAY NIGHTS ONLY 99 CENTS LIMIT 2 DESSERTS." Two things were now obvious—I was going to be a large man, and I had just been liberated from the Baptist church.

My buddies on the high school debate team were Jimmy and Bryce. Jimmy is a lawyer, living in Austin; he graduated from UT and UT Law. Bryce graduated from Notre Dame and the University Of Texas Law School. Then he became a major in the Air Force until, as he said, they found him one night at a rock concert dressed as Alice Cooper. He said the Air Force asked him to go into private practice. He did, in

Abilene. He died a few years ago at a time of his choice. I did not agree with his decision.

Oh, and that kid who sang rock and roll on the local TV station in Midland—the guy we called "Ooby Dooby"—the rest of the world called him Roy Orbison. My friends from the Baptist church—far as I know, they all turned out pretty good. Iris is a school teacher in East Texas, Benny is an associate pastor in Central Texas, and Tim became a CPA and successful businessman in California and retired early.

As for me, I learned that God is not a place or a building, but is inside each individual and is very personal. On Sundays my wife and I celebrate at the Chinese buffet, where we find all you can eat and no limits on desserts.

Now as far as the Baptist church is concerned, when my mother died in 2005, the people of the Baptist church were very kind, and at Christmas that year I sent a $1000 check to the church in her memory. It had been 11 months since she died. My thought was to make an annual gift at Christmas as a way of thanking the church in her memory. Well, they cashed the check, never bothered to say thanks, send a receipt or even a Howdy Dowdy. So, I think I am not only liberated from the Baptist church, I'm done with it.

GRADY PAUL

The first time I met Grady Paul was on the steps of a high school in Lubbock. He and his debate partner from Abilene had just whomped us guys from Midland pretty bad, and we sat on those steps for hours laughing as Grady held court.

Some people have God-given ability to do certain things—great athlete, singer, musician, etc. Grady had the ability to communicate. A few years later we ended up as debate partners in college. Our junior year we were very good.

Debate competition at the college level in those days, and probably still today, was very competitive. It didn't fill stadiums or show up on TV, but we had tournaments all across the country and at the end of the season, the best of the best (like college basketball) received an invitation to the national debate tournament.

Aristotle wrote that persuasion was accomplished with ethos, pathos, and logos—ethics, passion and logic. In order to prevail in debate, you had to have a comprehensive command of the debate topic. (A topic selected by some national group on a subject like free trade in North and South America). A debate team had to research the topic extensively and be prepared to debate both the yea and the nay of the same topic.

Grady Paul and I became a good debate team because of his ability to communicate and because I was the worker bee. At the end of the debate season of our junior year—think of it like some college basketball team sitting around waiting for the invitation to March Madness—well Grady Paul and I got the invitation to the National Debate Tournament. We were Cinderella, the small college, and we were going to the big dance.

But there was a problem. Remember I was the worker bee. Grady Paul was on scholastic probation—his GPA was under 2.0. Now the national debate tournament didn't care, but his university did, and the president of the university like a wicked stepmother said no you can't go. So another college was selected in our place.

People who knew Grady Paul would say he had all this talent but never used it to his potential. A few years go by and I have a new employer the American Heart Association and Grady Paul is working there, too. He is the Director of Planned Giving for the State of Texas. His job is to help people in estate planning. This is where people can leave part of their estate to a charity when they die. In order to be credible, Grady Paul became the worker bee. He knew more about estate planning than any lawyer or accountant had ever thought about at the time, and yet I don't think he ever finished college.

Grady Paul went on to work for several charities that are probably still benefiting today from his work. He died in 1991, from too much of living in the wrong places. I am thankful that I had the opportunity to tell him how proud I was of what he had accomplished.

At the celebration service of his life, many stories were told and eyes are filled with tears—tears of laughter, because that's what Grady Paul communicated best.

My favorite story happened like this:

In 1989, on a hot summer Friday an American Airlines jumbo jet filled to capacity with businessmen and women left New York heading to Dallas. They are grumpy—it's the end of the work week—they want out of those hot wet suits and into a cool dry martini. As the planes leaves JFK and banks south and west, Grady Paul is sitting in the cheap seats in the middle aisle. He looks around at the dour expressions on everybody's faces, so when the captain turns off the fasten seat belt sign.... Grady Paul stands up ... clapping his hands and sings just as loud as he can, "He's got the whole world ... in his hands ... come on everybody ... in his hands.... help me out on this one ... He's got the whole world in his hands." If you had been sitting in first class, you would have slowly heard this sound building from the back—a sound that you would soon join—"the whole world in his hands." By the time that plane landed in big "D", those people had sung up every song Grady Paul ever knew. People were laughing, shaking his hand, slapping him on the back, saying it was the best flight they had ever been on. It's too bad we can't sing on planes anymore.

CIVIL RIGHTS AND INTEGREATION

In the early 1960's there were civil rights marches, demonstrations, and riots across the country as integration slowly became a reality in America. When I graduated from Robert E Lee High School in 1964 there were no black kids. The only color we had was on the Confederate Flag. At college there were about 1500 students. Less than ten students were black; four were on the basketball team. There we no marches, demonstrations, or riots in my part of Texas.

In 1965 Hardin Simmons University had a pretty good basketball team. The coach was Lou Henson. He was an outstanding coach; later in his career he would lead New Mexico State and the University of Illinois and would take those programs to the NCAA final four. He had a long history of winning. I lived in the dormitory on campus called Anderson Hall. The black basketball players lived in the same dorm. One of our star players was a sophomore named Clarence. He was about 6' 5", so everybody called him Pee Wee. In those days the only television was in the lobby. There were several couches that seated three people and lots of chairs. About forty or so could watch TV if anything got our interest like a sporting event. One day I was watching TV, sitting on the end of one of the couches. I was the only kid in the lobby. Pee Wee comes over to the couch I am on, and stretches out next to me and says "Just came over to integrate this couch." I say, "Okay with me." The next day I am in an academic building and go into the men's room. Pee Wee is standing in the middle of a line of urinals. I go over next to him and say, "I just came in to integrate this bathroom." He looks at me, laughs and says "it's ok with me." I guess for our part integration had been achieved.

Later that week Pee Wee was playing in a game on campus. The little field house where our home games were played was full. It always was. The game was close and the crowd really got into it. A wife of one the administrators was especially excited. At one point she thought Pee

Wee was fouled. She yelled "Ref, that n***** just fouled our black guy." A pessimist would say she was a racist, and she probably was. An optimist might say she was making progress. Maybe she was. But Bob Dylan had it right. 'The times they are a changin'.

FLOWER POWER

It seems like it was yesterday. It was the calm before the
Storm and the storm was 1968. In January the North Vietnamese
began the Tet Offensive, which led to a larger conflict and seven more
years of war in Viet Nam. LBJ said, "I will not seek nor accept another
term." In April, Martin Luther King was killed. In June, Bobby
Kennedy was gunned down. On college campuses the SDS (students
for a democratic society) led demonstrations about the war and against
the government. Then in November, Richard Nixon was elected President … it was a storm.

But the summer before the storm, it was Flower Power, the Summer of
Love. Scott Mackenzie sang about going to San Francisco with a flower
in your hair. Today I live in Flower Mound and have no hair. In 1967,
I didn't go to San Francisco. It came to me in West Texas in the form
of twenty-year-old lass from San Francisco who had dark, golden hair
and beautiful smiling blue eyes.

I could say I was smitten, but that is such an old-fashioned term, and it
doesn't exactly capture what I remember of yesterday. But these old
dead brain cells don't function enough to express it better.

Now, some would say that my interest in this girl was because she was
the sister of my friend and debate coach, Maridell Fryar. That was not
true—she was an island all to herself—the Isle of Smitten. You may
think she was my first love, and you would be right, but not my
last—but those are stories I will tell later when this audience is older
and more mature.

On Thursday nights we would gather and watch Star Trek. Lou Ann
would sing the theme song. Never mind that the song was an instrumental—she sang it anyway. She also liked rock and roll, Jim Morrison

and the Doors. They would light her fire—but I couldn't—try as I would, and try I did.

Alas, she was in love with Bob. Well, what about Bob? What did he have that I didn't? OK, he was tall and good looking and lived in California. I was tall. And he wrote these dorky letters that he sent by air mail, except he wrote "fly it." What a jerk!

The summer turned into fall. Lou Ann and I would go out—movies, parks, hanging out at the Fryars' house not too far from the college campus. I could write her some poems or offer some witty conversation much superior to those dorky "fly it" letters—and then the big night came.

We went out and I was determined that this would be the Night that I would profess my true love to her. Now up to this Point, I had held her hand a few times, but still I was nervous. Being a college senior and being tall, I was confident I could win her over. And I tried, and then I tried another hour, and then two hours of begging went by, and the evening came to an end in the front yard of the Fryars' house. This beautiful girl came up to me, hugged me around my waist and kissed me on the lips, turned and walked into the house and said nothing. Dang, what did that mean?

I went by the house a couple of days later. Lou Ann wasn't there but Jack, her brother-in-law, was. Jack took me out on the front porch … and said "Terry, Bob is coming for Thanksgiving (it would have been kinder to have shot me but I don't think Jack had a gun) "I think you better just give up on Lou Ann and go after one of those other pretty girls on campus." I should have asked him who he had in mind. But I said "No, Jack, I love her." Jack said, "Well, Terry, she loves Bob … in fact she maybe having sex with Bob" (oh no, Jack … not sex!!!). Jack said, "Well, I'm not saying she is … I am just saying you have no chance."

And so it was the day Jack Fryar broke my heart. I would learn other lessons from Jack, lessons of life. My love for Jack and his wife would grow. And the other love—that summer before the storm—well, it had a hug and one kiss to last a lifetime.

GRANDMOTHERS

My grandmothers had great names for grandmothers. Minnie and Bessie, but we called them Granny and Mom Maw. Bessie was my mother's mother. My grandfather died when I was about two. It was an oil field accident. My father's father—never knew him, no one ever spoke of him, a mystery—only more confusing when my father discovered at age 40 that he had a half brother a little younger. So, that's all I know about him but I know a lot about Granny and Mom Maw.

THE JUNE BRIDE

Bessie lived in an old duplex in what used to be the center of Abilene. She rented out one half to supplement her income. Ever since I can remember, I thought that house was going to fall down, but it never did. She had some peach trees from which she used to make some of the best peach preserves ever eaten, and some big mesquite trees we would climb and make into a tree house. She had a chicken coop that provided Sunday dinner whenever we visited from Midland.

My brother Michael and two Cousins Sherri and Robert had to go on the other side of the house when Mom Maw went to get the chicken and wring its neck. We couldn't watch. Then my mother and her sisters Yvonne and Bobbie had to pluck the chicken. It was fried up and mighty good especially considering we were visiting Abilene and we didn't have to go to the Baptist church.

Bessie also had a boy friend—his name was Blue Eyes—at least that is what Mom Maw called him, so we did, too. The first time I met him had to be in the early 50's. Real nice fellow. Through the years I would sometimes be there when he came by after work. He would sit on the couch next to Bessie and drink a little whiskey with her, and they would talk real low and laugh.

In June, of her seventy—fifth summer Mom Maw announced to the family that she and Blue Eyes were getting married, and they did. It was a fun service. The family had gathered from here and there, and Blue Eyes a couple years her senior was a handsome groom, and Bessie was a beautiful, blushing bride. After the service I was talking to my dad and I asked him, "Why now? Why didn't she marry him 25 years ago?" Pop, said, "Oh, his wife died last month."

They were married for 4 years before cancer got him. They were happy, delightful years. The family gathered next at his funeral and listened to Willie Nelson singing "Blue Eyes Crying In The Rain." He was laid to rest in an old cemetery next to his first wife. When Bessie died a few years later, she was buried next to her first husband in the same cemetery. I am glad they are all together and I suspect they are, too.

HOW GRANNY GOT TO MILES, TEXAS

I knew my father was born in Dallas in 1919. I knew he was three month's premature and weighed one and half pounds. This was because his mother had the flu, in the epidemic of 1919 that killed tens of thousands of people across the country. Granny married a farmer named Smith in 1930 in Miles Texas, and I never heard any more about Mr. Smith. My first recollection of Granny was visiting her in Rowena, a little ways down the road from Miles. She lived in a small rock house across the street from the Rowena four-room school house. Next to the school house was the cafeteria, where Granny was the cook, and she was a great cook!

A few months before Granny died in 1980, I was visiting her and asked her "How did you get from Dallas to Miles." Well, she started laughing and told me this story:

In 1925, I was flat broke, living in Dallas with your father, trying to make ends meet as a waitress and cook at a diner. I was not doing too well. One day I saw an ad in the Dallas News that a man in Oklahoma had placed saying he was a widower with two daughters and needed a housekeeper and cook. He could pay $30 a month plus room and board. The ad said he was a mason, a member of the Masonic Lodge. She deduced that this meant he was a man of good character.

She wrote him a letter and said she could do what he needed, but there were two conditions. First, he had to pay for her train ticket to Oklahoma for her and her six-year-old son, and if it didn't work out, he had to pay for a train ticket to where ever she wanted to go. Well, he wrote back said that was acceptable, and he enclosed the train tickets to Oklahoma.

He picked her up in his wagon and took them to his farm. She told me that she fell in love with the two little girls. She did not like the farm and didn't like the man too much, but a deal was a deal. Three months go by. She notices that in her opinion he doesn't do much farming, and she sees some Indians around—who the man tells her not to worry about—but she does.

Then one day she finds a bunch of drunken Indians out behind the house. That's the day she finds out the man's real business. A couple of miles from the house he has a moonshine still—selling to all comers—mostly Indians. Granny said that while she felt sorry for the little girls, she could not raise her son in that place. It took a day or two of arguing with the man, but he finally agreed to live up to his end of the deal and buy her train tickets to wherever she wanted to go. She told him Miles Texas. That's where her family lived. He agreed to take her to town the next day to get a train.

So, Granny got her things, her son, got on the wagon, and went to town. The man owed her $30 for the month. When they got to town, he dropped her at the train station and said he had to go to the bank but would be back shortly with her money and her tickets. She said a couple of hours go by. She walks down to the bank. The man is nowhere to be seen. She says she had maybe two dollars and at her wits ends.

So, Granny goes into the general store, a gathering place, where several men were sitting around the pot belly stove drinking coffee. With one hand in the air and the other holding my dad's hand, at the top of her voice she yells, "IS THERE A MASON IN THE HOUSE?" She said there was silence in the store. Every eye was on her. "I SAID, IS THERE A MASON IN THE HOUSE?" The Masonic Lodge is a private, secretive society, especially in rural Oklahoma in 1925. But a man comes over to her and says, "Can I help you, lady?" She tells him the story and the deal she had made. He says, "Wait right here." She sees several men leave the store. An hour later they return—with $30 and two train tickets to Miles, Texas.

Twenty-five years after Granny died, Zoe and I are on a vacation in Lake City, Colorado. We are taking a tour of an abandoned gold Mine. There is a lady working in the gift shop a little younger than me, and she asks where we are from. We tell her Texas. She tells us she is from a small town out side of San Angelo. She says Rowena. I say really, you know my grandmother was the cafeteria cook for the school there many years ago. She looks at me and says, "Oh my god your grandmother was Miss Minnie I can see the resemblance."

MEETING, FALLING IN LOVE, AND BEING MARRIED TO DORIS DAY

Ok, so her real name is Zoe, and not Doris Day. But the first time I saw her, she looked every bit as good and a whole lot like Doris Day. She had the smile, the hair, the eyes, and the vixen innocent look that would tease you into thinking you were the only one in the room, even when you were. I knew right off the bat I was not in her league, but I smiled and nodded and said, "How are you?" I already knew she was major, and I was minor.

This game started in Houston. I lived in an apartment complex that had beautiful, almost tropical gardens in the center. It was called Tree Tops, and from my balcony I could look at tree tops and see the front door of Zoe's apartment. I liked to sit out there in the morning drinking coffee or in the afternoon drinking whiskey, and maybe get a glimpse of this Doris-Day-like creature coming and going. She looked good when she moved, even if she was standing still.

Shortly after moving in, I noticed in the late afternoon this older fellow maybe fifteen years older. A distinguished looking old coot, he would come, let himself in, and he never said a thing to me. I also knew two other things. This was a one bed room apartment and the name on mailbox was Z Quinton. He did not look like a Z to me, but then she looked like Doris Day. Now this old coot was not around all the time. I mean it wasn't like I was spying—much—but I did see him in the morning every now and then, in his bathrobe, getting the newspaper. Well, I had it all figured out. The old coot had a mistress that he visited occasionally. I couldn't blame him. So I just observed this for awhile.

Then one Friday afternoon I came home to find a note on my door. "Hi, my name is Zoe Quinton I live in the apartment across the way. My cat is on your balcony and I can't get her off. I am leaving soon for

San Antonio for the weekend. Can you please take care of my cat? My phone number is 454–6759. Thank you."

Well, I looked on the balcony and sure enough there is a really pissed off Siamese cat. I called the phone number, and she answered. She said, "thank god. I was about to leave." She came and got the cat. She really cared about that cat. She didn't mention the old coot. So now I had the name for the Z on the mailbox and I had the phone number.

On Memorial Day weekend I ask her out for a dinner date. She said yes, and the next two nights as well. She informed me that she was off to London for a week's vacation. I thought this might be a good thing for I am going broke taking her to dinner. Two days later so called me from London—collect. In those days it was cheaper to take her to dinner.

When she returns we become an item. She asks me "Why did it take you so long to ask me out?" So I tell her about the old coot. She says "Hell, that was my brother ... he is a Merchant Marine officer. He spends most of his time at sea, so he doesn't have a house. When he is in Houston, he sleeps on my couch and apparently ruins my love life."

Turns out it was her brother, but he is another story.

A few months later I get a better job offer to move to Dallas. I take it. Now, this is the point where relationships can go either way. But destiny, fate, the hand of the Almighty, I don't know—call it what you will. But this is what happened. A man named Lamar Muse bought three airplanes and started flying them between San Antonio, Houston, and Love Field in Dallas. Five minutes from my new apartment. On weekends you could fly for $13 dollars one way, cheaper than a collect call from London. Southwest Airlines they said they were the LOVVVE airlines—I thought that was an excellent point.

A couple of months later something else happened. Zoe's Company, Honeywell, had a downsizing and laid her off. So she decided to move to Dallas, get her own apartment and look for a job. Maybe I forget to mention that Zoe is also real smart. Understand, I had been hanging out with Doris Day, and in all truth I was not too focused on the brain. So her finding a good job in the banking industry was not a problem.

Life was good. She lived across the street. We both had new better paying jobs. So, in April of 1974. I got on my knees, told her I would love her forever, and I wanted her to marry me. She thought about that for two seconds, and said, "No, can't do it." Dang, end of discussion. But she said I could still take her out. A couple of months go by. In June she tells me, "I have found an apartment that I think would be good for us. Let's go look at it. If we move in July we can save some money. And I am thinking August 3 would be a good date for the wedding. Would that work for your family?"

"I thought you said no."

"Changed my mind."

"Well how do you know the invitation is still good?"

"Don't be ridiculous." So, I wasn't, and, I knew I had just been promoted to the major leagues.

The wedding is a small affair, about thirty or so family and friends at a small non-denominational chapel, naturally across from Love Field. It was set for 6 p.m. So we are standing in the parking Lot. It's about 105 degrees, and this guy pulls up in a station wagon, loaded with kids. He rushes up to the crowd, and says, "Do I have a wedding tonight?" Well, at that point it was nip and tuck. He hurries in, opening up the chapel, turning on the air conditioning. Zoe and her bridesmaid go into their little room. Jean would tell me later, "Zoe goes in, pulls off her hat, part of her dress and says, "Damn it I am sweating like a pig, wearing panty hose, and the ******* preacher doesn't show up. I don't know about this wedding!"

Zoe would tell anyone who would listen later. The only reason she went through with it was because my brother started playing the guitar, and he was so good that … Well, I guess music can sooth the savage beast and turn her into a gorgeous bride, and I have the pictures to prove it. Thanks, Michael.

The next day we head off for a honeymoon in Puerto Vallarta Mexico, but first we land in Monterrey, Mexico, with fire trucks and Federales everywhere. This was in a time when airplanes were being high jacked to Cuba. Let me tell you that was one quiet plane. When everything stopped moving, the captain finally told us it was only engine problems. That turned out to be the good news. The bad news is we had to wait for Mexicana Air to bring in another plane. Not to worry, they were opening up the bar in the terminal for us and there would be no charge. Then they ran out of ice, and then liquor.

We finally got to Puerto Vallarta thirteen hours late. However things were moving up. The bungalow we had was simply great with a western vista of the Pacific and a very private pool (If you get my drift). It was a wonderful six days.

This was my first trip to the interior of Mexico. I knew not to drink the water, so, of course, I drank lots of good ole bottled beer—great Mexican beer. It was a little hard getting it down for breakfast, but one does what one must.

Then it was almost time to leave. Six hours before the flight, and IT hit. They call it Montezuma's Revenge. I guess in a previous life I did something to Mr. Montezuma, because he was really hacked off at me. I don't know how I got on the plane. Zoe didn't want to sit with me, but she and the other passengers were very lucky that I didn't puke all over them. I did for the next week. I was so sick that when I got home, I opened my suitcase, got some aspirin, left the unfolded suitcase on the floor in the downstairs bedroom and went upstairs and stayed in bed a week. When I finally could come down, I discovered that the Siamese cat had used my suitcase, clothes and all, as the litter box for a week. But I was two weeks married to Doris Day.

One other thing happened while we were gone. Richard Nixon resigned.

UNDERSTANDING NEED

Gene and Mary Ellen were good friends of ours. On most Friday nights, we'd meet for drinks and dinner at various places in Oak Lawn, a part of Dallas that still has character. Gene liked coming to that part of town because as a kid he had a paper route there. He would tell us who use to live where.

Gene and Mary Ellen were about twenty years older than Zoe and me. Gene was a senior executive for a major oil company, and he made substantially more money than the two of us put together. Maybe because of the age difference, maybe the money difference, or maybe just because of the way he was, he would not let me pick up a check for anything, and it was dang right embarrassing. One Friday night, at an up-scale Italian restaurant, when the check came and Gene grabbed it as usual, I told him the story of need that my friend Jack Fryar had related to me.

When I first met Jack, he was an English teacher at Midland High School. One of the courses he taught was honors English. On the first day of school, he would tell that class, that everyone who finished the course would make an A, because that was the ONLY kind of grade acceptable in HIS honors course.

Jack's parents were farmers. They had about six hundred acres outside of Stanton, Texas about twenty miles from Midland. Jack said on most weekends they would come to Midland and bring loads of fresh produce from the farm and thrust it on him and Maridell. Well, Jack didn't like this at all. He would tell his parents that he and his wife were both successful school teachers completely capable of taking care of their family. But the next weekend came and another load of produce would be delivered.

One cold night before Christmas, a faulty gas heater went awry, and Jack parents died. Jack told me that as he looked back on those events, he finally understood that those loads of produce were given to him not because he needed them, but because his parents needed to give them. I looked Gene in the eye and said, "Gene, I need to pick up that check." Slowly Gene passed the check over to me.

Not long after this Mary Ellen began her second battle with breast cancer. A fight she would lose. One evening over drinks Gene told me that the chemo was making her really sick, and he had heard that smoking pot might help. He said, "Terry I need to do anything I can to help her, but I don't know how or where to get it." Not surprising he was a senior exec of a big oil company. I said, "Gene, I don't know either, but I might know someone who does."

I called Grady Paul. The next day, a guy named Mark brought me a bag of marijuana. This was my one and only drug deal. I gave it to Gene. Gene said, "How much do I owe for this?" Well, that was the second check Gene never picked up. I think we both understood need.

One last note. The most famous librarian to graduate from Midland Lee High School is Laura Welch. She married a guy named George W. Bush. But the library at Lee High School is named after Jack Fryar.

BROTHER IN LAW

I must admit I was dubious about Zoe's claim about the guy in her apartment being her brother, turns out he was. The first time I met him he visited my apartment for a spaghetti dinner. Before dinner, I offered him a beer. He just laughed and said, "No thanks." I pointed out that I had a full bar if he didn't like beer. Again, laugh, and "No thanks." With dinner I, of course, offered some really good wine (at least it had a cork in it). Again, laugh, "No thanks." I am thinking, this guy is a Merchant Marine, and he doesn't drink. Zoe tells me the next day he doesn't, at least not in the last nine years.

Charles left home in 1944 when he was fifteen to join the Merchant Marines, see the world, and became a drunk. I heard a preacher say once "No one ever takes the first drink and intends to become an alcoholic." Well, Charles's intentions aside he did become an alcoholic.

When he was thirty six years old, and almost dead, he quit drinking. He joined Alcoholic Anonymous. For the rest of his life he attended meetings and organized chapters all over the world. He would tell me, "I quit drinking, then I quit smoking, but I will never quit women."

Now the rest of the family didn't quit. When we went out, and people took turns buying drinks, Charles took his turn with a coke while buying the rest of us single malts, blended blends, or straight up over the rocks. He never complained. It surely wasn't fair, us paying for 50 cent cokes, and him paying for $5 glasses of booze. But I think he thought that was just the price of being sober.

In AA a birthday means one year sober. Charles had thirty six birthdays. He died one evening in April after finishing a workout in his gym. I always wondered if he knew he was going to die that night ... would he have gone to the bar or the gym.

His funeral was interesting. Six hundred sober drunks came to hear stories of Charles. Most of them wanted to know what he was like when he was drinking, as they had only known him sober. The facts are this high school dropout became a Captain in the Merchant Marines. It takes years of schooling and experience to reach that status. A very smart man. He traveled all over world several times. It certainly occurs to me now; he deserved a standing ovation.

AIRPLANES

This is my favorite story about Southwest Airlines. A few years ago (when I actually worked and traveled) I went from Dallas to Houston for a day of business meetings. I had an early flight, about 7:30 a.m., out of Dallas Love Field. It was in the fall, and the day was overcast and drizzly. The plane was almost full of business travelers. In those days, Southwest had both in the rear of the plane and in mid-cabin three seats that faced forward and three seats that faced the rear—six people facing each other on each side of the aisle—for a total of twelve in the same row.

These seats (to the experienced Southwest passengers) were Choice, because they had more room and in the morning you got coffee first and in the afternoon you got booze first. Often, because you were facing your fellow passengers, conversations of all sorts developed particularly in the afternoon after the drinks came.

On this flight, I was in the back, along with other business folks and a father and his two kids, a boy about ten and a girl about five or six. As the twelve of us were taking our seats, the father sat in the middle, with the little girl getting the window seat. The flight attendant remarked to the young man, "Oh, is this a school holiday?" (It was midweek.) The father said, "No, we have to attend a funeral in Houston." The flight attendant said, "I am so sorry."

Well, on this dreary drizzly morning we take off and go through a heavy cloud deck probably 10,000 feet or so. It seems like it took forever to get through the clouds. But, as many of you who travel know, a remarkable thing happens when the plane breaks through those clouds. We were traveling east, and the sun was still rising.

All of a sudden the dreary, drizzly day is beneath you and the sun fills the cabin like a miracle. It's a new world. The little girl grabs her father and exclaims for all to hear "Daddy, maybe we can see Grandpa up here." Well the dad hugs the little girl, tears coming down his cheeks and for the rest of the flight we grizzly veterans of business travel—not a dry eye in the group—we contemplate what this dad's conversation must have been like the night before.

CATS

When a guy like me marries someone like Zoe one of two things happen; the girl either dumps him, or she finds out that he is trainable. What is not trainable is a cat. The Siamese cat was named Holly after Holly Golightly, the Audrey Hepburn character in "Breakfast At Tiffany's." Holly liked only one person walking this planet. Her favorite place was Zoe's butt. Most evenings Zoe would drop off to sleep on the couch watching TV with a Half-full wine glass clutched in one hand, and Holly perched on her rear end.

Now here is where the training comes in. First, never take the wine glass from you wife's hand if she is sleeping, because it will wake up her and that will irritate the cat. This does lead to disaster. Second, never approach your wife's derriere in a romantic mood when a cat is on it. This leads to complete disaster, and could even involve stitches.

We have had several cats over the years. The most we ever had were four ... Janet and Eloise, Oscar and Felix. She wanted more, but I pointed out that was the legal limit for one household in Dallas and I had attended some courses at the University of Texas Law School, which sort of made me an officer of the court and I simply could not violate the law.

Today we have two cats. Both were adopted from rescue leagues. One is a mostly black tortoise shell with little splashes of yellow. The rescue people named her Hallie, because they rescued her at Halloween from people out to do her harm. We added the name Berry, because the week we got her the famous Ms. Berry won the academy award. Hallie is one sweet cute little girl. But she is not trainable either—she thinks the kitchen sink is the sand box.

The other cat is pure white and very pretty. She was recently put on the FBI's list of terrorists. The name given her by the nice lady who was fostering her prior to her adoption was Leah. She didn't seem like a Leah to us. The day after we adopted her, Zoe talked with her foster mom on the telephone. The lady mentioned that they had named her after Leah, the young, beautiful daughter of the character 'Bloody Mary' in the movie "South Pacific." Since "South Pacific" is one of Zoe's favorite movies and she knows all the musical lyrics and most of spoken dialog, she recognized the lady's error immediately. The character she was thinking of was Liat, not Leah. So, Leah became Lucy. Actually, Lucy Ricardo, she is both beautiful and dingy. Any one who comes into our house is immediately warned about Lucy … you can look but you better not touch.

The death of a pet is always a sad thing, particularly for a couple who forgot to have children. On our small cul de sac we call the Rock Farm. I once circulated this notice to our family of dear friends.

AN OBITUARY

On the day that the King of the Cowboys died, so did the Big "O." Oscar Broxson Kitty Kat, 1985–1998, disguised as a tabby, was truly an "Oster Toaster," a mythical Himalayan wolf cat. The only way to tell was to look deep into his green eyes and see the sparkle that revealed his true identity. Many have asked how a wolf cat from the high Himalayas ended up on Turtle Creek in 1985, where Zoe found him and his brother, Felix. There are two answers to this question. One, we don't know. Two, it's a myth. Oscar was a remarkable chow cat, first in line and last to leave.

The way he loved the Colonel's chicken made Zoe think that one of the secret spices had to be Cat Nip. Today the Rock Farm is a little quieter.

THE REAL MR. BROXSON

Whenever any one called me Mr. Broxson, I always thought, they meant my father. I guess every kid who knew their father thought the same thing. Getting the Mr. before your last name is something that takes a lifetime to earn. We called him Bill. His real name was Gilvin Cooper Broxson. I have heard that he once was called Little Bill as a kid. But who was big Bill. Heck if I know. Everybody outside of the family called him Gil.

When H. Ross Perot became famous in the 60's, I told my father he should change his name to G. Cooper, and maybe he would be a billionaire too. But he didn't and so we weren't. We were middle class America.

My father sold life insurance in the oil patch that was West Texas for most of his adult life. At age forty, he decided to learn Morse code, so he could become a licensed amateur radio operator. Trust me that is not easy to do at age forty. Mother made his birthday cake that year with "Life begins at 40!" He said it sure does and I am going to be a HAM (short for amateur radio operator).

My brother and I would also call him the old man. The old man passed his test and got his radio license. His call signal was WA5FDL. When radio hams talk to each other they identify themselves with their call signal. They also use phonics to make sure the other ham got the right call signal. My father would do it like this. "This is WA5FDL, that's whiskey able five fast dangerous lover." When he got older he changed it. "This is whiskey able five fat, dumb, and lazy."

Amateur radio was an all consuming hobby for the old man. He had the ability to stay up till late into the night drinking Mr. Jim Beam's whiskey and talking to people all over the world. He also had the ability to get up early in the morning and start all over again before going to work.

One such early morning occurred on a Friday June 11, 1965. He was listening to his radio when he heard another ham from Sanderson, Texas report there was a disaster in the town. It had been hit with a terrible flash flood. In fact is was a wall of water fifteen feet high that had roared down a canyon and smashed into the town. Many homes and business were destroyed and twenty eight people lost their lives. The ham said they needed help.

Sanderson is a small town in the Big Bend area of Texas. Well, the old man loaded his portable equipment and took off. For the next forty eight hours he would not sleep. There was no electric service or phone service. So he set in his car with the engine running to power his portable radio. His car became the local news information agency. He would broadcast news of survivors to anxious loved ones all over the country. He received a citation for his work.

When he turned sixty-five he bought one of the first personal computers, so he could capture all the poems he had written in his life and he wrote a lot of them. This is only remarkable, because at the time, my brother in law, who really is a Bill, worked for IBM and told me they were not sure these p/c's things were going to sell, because they didn't know what people would do with them.

If my father had high expectations of me, he never said. But when I was some how accepted to a college, he said he would pay for it. One time when I was home, when I was nineteen, he was feeling his oats, or his whiskey or something. He got on my case about how good I had it, going to college on his money "When I was nineteen I graduated high school, a year late because I had to lay out a year to work the farm." My mother simply looked at him, and said "When I was nineteen, I had been married a year!" He never brought that subject up again. He did pay every penny for me to go to college.

When we closed out the family home, I found a book, "RUDYARD KIPLING'S VERSE." Inside the front cover in blue ink it says, "Thanks Dad, for four years of debt free college, Terry." I do not remember giving him the book, but I am glad I did.

The first page of this book is a poem he wrote in 1986. I find it ironic, twenty years later that I am kind of doing the same thing. What follows are two poems of his. The first was written while he served in the Army Air Corps during WWII, the second was written toward the end of his life.

ARMY WINGS

A far off sound
Of motor tune,
A shadow cast
Against the moon.

A moment here
And then gone by,
Into the distance
Of the sky.

A fading sound,
A dimming light.
It's Army Wings
In the night.

BULLSHIT

Bullshit
The most spoken and unspoken word,
In the language of mankind.
How many times have you said it
To your silent rage,
When discretion was the
Better part of Valor?

At one time or another
Bullshit can describe more things,
Than any other word
In the language of mankind:
Husbands,
Wives,
Bosses,
Waiters,
Headlines,
Ads in papers,
TV shows,
Society dames,
Income tax,
Braggers,
Salesmen,
Politicians,
And fish stories.

Bullshit describes
Many things,
But not
Mother,
Money,
God.

JIM McCORMICK

When Jim McCormick died in February of 1995, there were easily a thousand people at his service. There were celebrities, rich powerful movers and shakers of Dallas, and a whole lot of folks who just admired the heck out of the guy. He died a wealthy man. It's not just about money. He was wealthy in family, friends and kindness. But it didn't start that way. He told me he came from the wrong side of the tracks in Ennis, Texas, a small town southeast of Dallas.

The story of Jim McCormick was a "long complicated struggle to try to do the right thing." Those were his words not mine and I could never do justice to his life story. So, here is my story about the time that my friend and business associate, Leland, and I got off an elevator after Jim had rolled his wheelchair out of a meeting we had on some unremembered business issue of no lasting importance.

You need to know a few things about Jim in order to understand why I remember the conversation with Leland on the elevator. In World War II Jim was trained as a B-17 bomber pilot. In the class was an older fellow named Clark Gable, they would become friends. Jim's plane was shot down. He was a POW, but he didn't talk about it. After the war, he was consumed by his love for Barbara and his need to get an education. He claims they lived in a converted chicken coop while he got his degree from SMU. He got a job with an investment banking company in Dallas. Jim, the company he worked for and their clients would do very well over the years to come.

In the early 50's before polio was defeated, polio attempted to defeat Jim. It put him in an iron lung for months. Jim said he would lay in the damn piece of ****. Hopeless until he said "God, I will make a deal with you. If you let me get out of this machine for one hour, I will never ask you for another thing," and he got out of the machine for an hour. Then Jim said, "tell you what God if you would let me sit in that chair over there for a few minutes, I will never ask you for another thing." He got to sit in the chair.

He thought, "You know God, there is a wheel chair over there, and if I could just sit in that wheelchair someone could roll me down the hall, and I promise you I will never ask for another thing." And so it was. Then Jim said. "God if I could just roll that wheelchair with my own hand, I swear I will never ask for another thing." Well you know what happened.

I don't know how many more conversations he had with God. I know it was a lot—with two canes Jim was able to walk for forty years until an accident and age put him back into a wheelchair. He had two kinds. One was motorized, and also a smaller chair. On the back of both chairs was a sign—LIFE IS GREAT!

So, as Leland and I got off the elevator after our meeting, with Jim rolling his chair briskly ahead of us, Leland turned to me and said, "Terry I don't know whether to offer to push Mr. McCormick's wheel chair or not. What do you think?" I simply told him the truth. "Hell no, he made a deal with God!" Jim deserved a standing ovation.

LARRY

I don't remember the first time I met Larry. He was probably ten or so. He is the youngest son of Zoe's brother, Bill. Although this story is about Larry, you might need to know a little about Bill.

The short of it is he grew up in a poor family in Beaumont, Texas. His brother, Charles, ran off to sea. That happened when Bill was fourteen, and then his mother announced she was pregnant with the first of two sisters for Bill and Charles. Somehow Bill got to Texas A&M University and received a degree. He also received an invitation to go to Korea and serve Uncle Sam.

So, it's not surprising that Bill, who had four kids of his own, would teach his kids self reliance and accountability. Besides he was an executive with IBM, so he was used to having things his way. The first two boys got degrees from Arizona State and Oklahoma State. One of them got a master's degree. And, those boys paid for their schooling, the details of which will have to remain a family secret because the statute of limitations may not be up on all the financial transactions.

But Larry was a different matter. I don't know if he graduated high school, or just got thrown out, but at least he got out. By the standards of young ladies, Larry was cute, and he was fun, and when it came to accountability … well Larry couldn't spell it. On the other hand, he enjoyed life.

For most of his adult life, Larry has lived in Dallas and worked as a tile contractor. From my perspective, his typical day for about fifteen years was work a little, hit the bars, hit on the women, run out of money and go home. His idea of planning ahead was to pull his hand out of his pockets, and say "Damn, I am out of money!" A long-term relationship was a three-day holiday weekend. Larry was a happy camper, but not his brothers or his dad. Both of his brothers were married and had good jobs. They were raising families, and they thought he should be more responsible. Larry was raising hell and enjoying every bit of it.

When Larry needed to buy a pickup truck, Bill had to co-sign the loan. At the bank in Dallas, the loan officer carefully looked over Larry's credit history and looking at Bill said, "Sir, do you know what it means to co-sign a loan?" Bill assured him he had been around the block a time or two. Larry did pay off the loan.

I should mention at this point that Larry is a real good tile contractor. He has always been willing to give the family the "good guy price."

One time Zoe and I were going on a vacation, and we are going to be gone a week. Zoe wanted some tile work for the bathroom. Larry offers to do the work while we are gone. He says he will stay at our place, do the work, and take care of the cats and only charge us for materials. I say, "Larry that sounds great, and I will also leave the keys to my car if you need it."

The car was a Mercedes 450SL. What the hell was I thinking? I probably wasn't sober. We come back, the tile looks good, the car is fine, and then I notice it has a new tire. Larry explains that he and two buddies are out cruising one night, looking for ladies. I am thinking, "Wait, this is a two-seat convertible, did he say two buddies, and did they find any ladies?" Larry says, "We had a flat on Central Expressway about two in the morning, we couldn't get the jack to work, so we got you a new tire."

When Larry was thirty-five a miracle happened. Her name is Connie. In April of that year, Larry's family came to our backyard and, with a hundred other people, witnessed the unthinkable—Larry Married!

Let's fast forward a little. Today, Larry does not work for a tile contractor—he owns the business. He has a son starting the first grade. He owns property, and his credit is good. On Sundays, when he used to have to figure out which bar he would go to so he could watch football and place bets, he now takes the family to church. Larry also owns an old 1960's Rolex watch—the next repair job is duct tape. Larry tells me he wants to trade it in on a new one, but Connie needs something for the house or his son Brennan needs something for school, or the business needs something.

So, one evening Zoe and I are talking about Larry. We note that it is really great how Larry's life has turned out. He has gone from being the Mothers Against Drunk Driving and Mothers Protecting their Daughters worst nightmare to their best example. Well, we decide Larry should be recognized for this. He comes over one evening, and I ask him if he wants to trade in his old Rolex for what's in this box I am holding. He says he does. In the box is a new Rolex Submariner. My buddy Mel at Dallas Watch and Jewelry gives me $600 for Larry's old one. Larry made a good deal.

A few weeks later he comes by the house. He tells me how proud he is of the watch. He says, "You know the things I value the most in life are first my kid, then my watch, then my wife, and then my business." I am now thinking, okay maybe he's not done, but at least he has made a lot of progress.

One last thing about Bill—his first wife died from breast cancer. She was the mother of his four kids. I never met her, but I was told she was a jewel. I did know his second wife. I wondered, "What was he thinking?" I guess he was thinking the same thing. What happens next is what Bill calls an earthquake. The rest of us call it a divorce. This earthquake swallows up a whole bunch of his long green in the bank. But then Zoe comes to his rescue, not with money, but with her best friend Debby. Debby didn't bring any money either, but she has enriched his life for over fifteen years. Now you can't spend enrichment because it's too valuable.

PRESIDENTS AND POLTICANS

A baby boomer by definition was born after World War II. The war ended in 1945, so the country celebrated by making lots of babies beginning in 1946. If you don't know, the war ended in stages. First was VE day for Victory in Europe. That was in May of 1945 and then VJ day for Victory over Japan was in September. Since I was born in April of 1946, some quick math means my parents decided to celebrate after VE day—couldn't wait for VJ day.

So the first President of my life was Harry Truman. Rush Limbaugh once said, "Truman decided to drop the bomb and two things happened, a war ended and we won." There was a third thing, too. The World did not want to see it again. Thankfully, we have not. But I don't know about the next sixty years.

Ike was the first President I ever saw on TV. I think it was in 1953. Midland didn't even have a TV station, but that did not stop my father from getting a TV. He didn't have an antenna though. Mr. McClure across the street had an antenna on top of a telephone pole, but he didn't have a TV. Strange neighborhood. So my dad and his neighbor strung a wire across the street and we got a snowy, fuzzy picture from Lubbock that showed President Eisenhower making a speech, and baby boomers became the first television generation.

In 1960, in junior high, I was a member of the new Frontier Club. That would be Youth for Kennedy. I was in algebra class at 1:15 on November 22, 1963 when Mr. Hines Principal of Lee High School turned on the loud speakers to let us listen to the radio reports from Dallas.

Of course, being a Texan, I was proud to see LBJ become President. And, then it became a disaster. The War. The Great Society that wasn't. Only to be followed by Richard Nixon. The best thing that happened in this stretch of years is that Gerald Ford pardoned Richard Nixon and saved the country a whole bunch of time and money.

Jimmy Carter was the last Democrat I ever voted for. That was in 1976. I voted for Anderson in 1980. It is amazing to me, now, to look back on those seventeen years and think about how bad our Presidents were. In my opinion only Ford stands out. The War ended and he put Nixon behind us.

I voted for Reagan in 1984, the last time I voted for a Republican. He was clearly the best president since FDR. I think that George Herbert Walker Bush was doing pretty well. But he did not finish the work. And now look at the quagmire that is Iraq. It might have been different. We will never know.

So, Jim McCormick and I both voted for Ross Perot in 1992. The first of my baby boomer generation gets elected President. Bill Clinton is certainly a likeable enough guy. The only problem is that he has the morals of a billy goat. And he thinks raising taxes is a good thing. I don't.

Now we have George W. Bush, a fellow baby boomer, from Midland, married to a girl I graduated high school with. I even gave his campaign $500 dollars in 2000, but only because Lyda Hill asked me. This puts me on the Christmas card list. I got a Christmas card from George and Laura for four years. In 2004, Lyda didn't ask for any more money, so I have not gotten anymore Christmas cards.

I think it was Teddy Roosevelt, who said, "Surround yourself with good people and stay out of their way." Clinton surrounded himself with the wrong people and got in the way. George W. just needed better people. I guess he didn't know any .I do wonder why anyone wants the job. Smart people all over the world are going to be critics, even dumb ones like me.

FAMILY REUNIONS

I guess that family reunions can either be stressful or fun depending on whether you are the parent or the kid. Since Zoe and I never had kids, they were always fun and sometimes educational. The first family reunion I attended was what my father called "the world-wide family reunion of the cousins." It was held in Ballinger, Texas, at the city park. This is not too far down the road from Miles and Rowena.

The first "reunion of the cousins" had some great educational value to me. Those who knew me years ago recall that I had red hair. What hair my father had was black; so were mothers and my little brother's. Growing up everybody asked me "Where did you get that red hair?" Heck, I was a little kid. How was I supposed to know? As it turns out Granny was the youngest of thirteen kids. So when all the cousins showed up, there were about 250 people at the reunion. Seventy-five or so had red hair.

The food was great. There was bar-b-q, fried chicken, twenty-seven different kinds of salad, and at least thirty-eight desserts. And of course barrels of ice tea. These were Baptists.

Zoe's family reunions were a little different, but just as fun and educational. First they were smaller, and they lasted longer. These events occurred over a long weekend at Crystal Beach, just north of Galveston. Zoe's mother and father had started the tradition. A beach house would be rented. Attendance varied each year from fifteen to thirty-five depending on how many cousins showed up, and various boy friends, girl friends, or other friends.

Now here is where the educational part comes in. Brother-in-law Bill told me from the start that the only way to survive one of these gatherings was to start drinking beer about ten in the morning and pace yourself with about one an hour. At 4 pm you should switch to vodka, scotch, whiskey or other adult beverage of choice. You should drink that until you passed out hopefully in a bed. He assured me that this was the only way to avoid any disputes involving any of the attendees that might arise on these occasions. His point being if a dispute arose, at the time you would not care, and the next morning you would not remember.

Bill had learned this from his father Charlie, who would sit in a beach chair all day and pay his grandkids a quarter to bring him a beer. This became the foundation for their college fund.

Bill did a have good point about the bed. These beach houses usually had four to six beds. The rules were simple. Any grandmother got a bed. Next, the oldest married couple got a bed. If you paid for the house you got a bed. At this point, the beds were gone so next, the oldest single people got whatever couches were available or slept in the car of their choice. Kids always got the floor.

Since Charles, the older brother, spent most of his time traveling the sea as a Merchant Marine, he did not always make these reunions. When he did he made this observation: "This looks like a drinking contest." Since he was sober, I learned to look at him as the winner.

One year when Larry was about thirteen my buddy Carl decided to join us. Carl had recently started his medical practice in Abilene, and he needed a break—go to the beach, blow some soot. On the first night of the reunion, Carl and Larry stay up until 3 a.m. talking. They are the last two to turn in. The next day Larry tells me, "I really like Carl; he is the first adult to talk to me like an adult." Later I am talking to Carl and say, "You really impressed young Larry last night." "Oh" he says, "That's who I was talking to. I had so much scotch; I couldn't remember who it was, or what I said." I guess Bill was right.

Another educational point was about the food. Now in West Texas, if it was not beef or chicken, and if it was not grilled or battered and fried, it was not eaten. Zoe's family tied a long string to a chicken neck, threw it in the bay, slowly brought it in and then another family member with a net on a long pole would net a crab that was hanging onto the chicken. I had never seen this before; there was no water where I came from.

These crabbing expeditions would take several hours and require great quantities of beer. These people would catch about a hundred or so of these crabs and add them to something called gumbo, which looked like a bunch of dead sea creatures swimming in soup. They all ate it and claimed it was delicious. I just figured they were too drunk to know what they were eating. I had a ham sandwich.

ANNIVERSIARIES AND BIRTHDAYS

Wedding anniversaries were always celebrated when I was growing up. My mother and father were married on February 22, 1941. This was also George Washington's Birthday. I just thought the whole country celebrated along with us. From the time I entered the first grade until I graduated high school, our family finances went from just about poor to firmly in the middle class.

But on February 22 of each year, we got to go to the Blue Star Inn. The Blue Star Inn was just the fanciest place to dine in Midland. If there were fancier places to go, well, we could not afford them. A Chinese Family owned the Inn, but I don't think they served Chinese food. If they did, we were not allowed to eat it. We could only eat Texan (bar-b-q or fried) and of course Mexican. Any other ethnic food was out of the question. But they had great steaks and, of course, excellent chicken fried steak with cream gravy.

On this annual occasion Jack and Maureen and their kids from Odessa joined us. We would all dress up in our Sunday best. Mother and Maureen would wear gowns. My father and Jack wore suits. There were flowers and gifts given. Wine was ordered for everybody over twenty-one, except my mother of course. Dad and Jack would smoke cigars, right there in the restaurant. It was an event. It turns out Jack and Maureen were married on February 23, 1941. My mother and father had fifty-one anniversaries. I believe Jack and Maureen celebrated forty-eight of those with them. When Maureen passed away she and Jack had had sixty-five anniversaries.

My parents met Jack and Maureen during WWII in Coffeyville, Kansas. Being a baby boomer of the WWII generation, I, of course wanted to hear heroic exploits of battles like I saw in the movies. So, I was disappointed to learn my father was a staff sergeant at an air base. Along with his other duties he ran the camp bowling alley, right dab in the middle of the United States. I could not think of a safer place in the world during those years. I would find out after he died that the government rules provided that widows who only had one son were allowed to serve state side. He did his part at home.

Anniversaries for Zoe and me are a lot less formal. But the occasion must be marked in some manner or I will be in big trouble. On the seventeenth year, I gave her seventeen presents each wrapped individually. On the 25th anniversary we had a grand party. I asked three of my friends to make an after-dinner speech. I asked them several months ahead of time and assigned them a topic related to marriage.

We invited about thirty-five people for "Celebrating 50 years of marriage that's 25 for him and 25 for her." After dinner, Carl was the first to speak. His topic was "Who is in charge?" He started like this:

Gather 'round in this gorgeous garden spot,
And hear what's true and what is not.
Settle back in this bloom-filled'd yard,
And learn from me just who's in charge.

He went on for ten more minutes and concluded with this:

Walk inside this house and carefully look 'round.
You'll see the walls with cat art abound.
Terry and Zoe's lives are like two hearts entwined,
And the common thread in their fabric is, indeed, feline.

So, who would you say is in charge of this house?
Well, it isn't a dog, and it isn't a mouse.
Not knowing must mean that you are from Mars.
It's plain to me that the cats are in charge!

Robert was next. His topic was "Advice, the Good, the Bad, and the Ugly". He offered up several pieces of advice, but my favorite was this:

"I had a physician client tell me that when he started out working he worked for an old general practitioner in Grapevine. He was doing this as part of his medical school training. On the last day he worked there, the old fellow called him back to his private office, sat him down and offered this bit of advice. The key to a happy and successful life consisted of complying with three simple rules: First, stay married to your first wife. Second, never live in a house only a doctor can afford. Third, only borrow half the money the bank will loan you."

Robert concluded by saying, "if you doubt the wisdom of this advice, consider that a recent article in USA Today reported that 75% of millionaires in this country have been married to their first wife for more that 25 years. So if you've achieved that financial milestone, you know why! And if you haven't, you know at least one of the things you did wrong."

Joe was the last speaker, and remember that our anniversary is the first week of August. Joe's topic was "Living in Texas Ain't half bad." This is how he starts:

"Terry and Zoe I can't tell you how much I appreciate the opportunity to share this evening with you. This hot evening. This really hot evening. This ****ing hot evening. What comes next—raining toads?

"I was born and raised in New York, which makes me a natural nemesis of native Texans, a Yankee. Moreover, I have no intentions of going back to New York, which makes me a Damn Yankee.

"I remember as if it was yesterday my arrival in Texas. It was the summer of '78 when I drove into Lubbock Texas, a city whose motto is 'If you like horizon, you're home'. You have to be concerned about a city that advertises tractor pulls in the Society Page of the paper.

"But life in Lubbock was not half bad. Because in Lubbock I discovered a unique Texas institution-the drive through liquor store. I thought to myself 'finally a state that caters to the drunk on the go'."

Joe went on for several more minutes. He was so funny that people asked me later if he was a professional comedian. No, he is a PHD ergonomic engineer and brilliant. The fact is all three were brilliant. That is why I asked them.

My most remembered birthday as a kid was when I was ten or eleven. Midland had a TV station by then, KMID, Channel 2. They had a program called "Two Gun Playhouse." The movies were all old westerns from the 30's and 40's. It was sponsored by Meltzer's Milk. The station invited you write in, in twenty-five words or less, why you drank Meltzer's milk. Of course we drank Borden's. But that didn't seem to matter. If your entry was selected, you got to come on TV, and Jerry Blair would present you with two genuine fake cap guns with holsters.

Well, my mother seemed to know why I liked Meltzer's, even if I didn't. That is how I got my cap guns for my birthday that year. The only problem was that Jerry Blair (the local news, weather and sports announcer) was on vacation. So Uncle Eddie filled in. Turns out Uncle Eddie later goes out to Hollywood and becomes Edward Platt, a pretty good actor. He was in lots of movies and was best known as "Chief" in TV's "Get Smart".

My birthday for most of the rest of my life would go pretty much unnoticed. This probably explains how I got past sixty. Zoe's birthday is a different matter. I am not saying she thinks it ought to be a

National Holiday—she would probably settle for a State Holiday. On her thirtieth birthday, her friend Jean gave her a cake with thirty candles. The cake was made in a perfect image of a woman's naked rear end. The inscription said "29 MY ASS."

Twenty years later I invited eighty-five people to come to our new house to celebrate "ZOE BROXSON, THE FIRST 50 YEARS." Ten years later, they were invited to "CELEBRATE ZOE'S SECOND 30th BIRTHDAY."

THE CUL DE SAC

In 1993 we built a house in Flower Mound, just west of Dallas and east of Ft. Worth. The only other house we ever owned was a townhouse in the center of Dallas in an area known as Oak Lawn. We called it South Highland Park. If you know the area then you know why. We sold that house after fifteen years. I keep records of every transaction for tax purposes. My accountant, after reviewing my records, said, "Terry, you are the only person I ever knew in the city of Dallas to make a profit on a townhouse." It was $80.

Our place was the fourth house to be constructed on the cul de sac. There would be a fifth added later. I met one of my neighbors right away. Her name was Kathy, and she had a cute six-month-old surprise on her hip named Colleen. I say a surprise because, like Zoe, Colleen came along fourteen years after her brothers. Turns out Kathy's husband Robert was on the debate team with me in college, and of course he knew Grady Paul.

Our next door neighbors are Pam and Ray. Across the street is where Sid and Sherrill live. I did not formally meet them until Zoe's 50th birthday party. I went over to each house and introduced myself and said, "There are going to be about forty cars in the cul de sac on this Saturday night; it is going to be noisy. I would really prefer you come join us, instead of being mad at us. Besides this way you will know who to be mad at and why." They did. There is an old saying about not being able to choose your family, but you can choose your friends. With neighbors, you gotta get lucky. We got lucky.

Pam was a Vice President of Personnel for a big Dallas-based company and Ray was a lawyer, a litigator for the IRS. When I found this out I thought, "Lord what have we done? Good thing I keep records." Turns out Pam is a real sweetheart, and Ray was after big oil companies and not neighbors.

Sid was a high mucky-muck Marketing Director for an international company. In short, he was a super salesman. Sherrill is an extremely elegant homemaker, with an extremely elegant home. Their home is spotless. The only time our house is spotless is when a fine layer of dust covers the spots.

Now we don't have favorites, but you should know that Sid and Sherrill are cat people. So, when they are away, we take care of the cats, the squirrels, plants etc. And they do the same for us. In fact they take better care of our place than we do. Now that Zoe and I are retired, we plan to travel more. This way our place will look better.

Robert has owned several businesses that he has sold. He is an investor, golfer and stable hand. Kathy is a nurse and a mother with two sons in their 20's. Colleen is about to be a teenager and rides horses. Robert and Kathy were the first to sell their home. They only moved a few miles away so we still see them. But we have told them that a screening committee should have been set up. Remember, with neighbors, you gotta get lucky. Sometimes, you don't.

Our cul de sac has seen some fun times. Pam, Ray, Sid, Sherrill, Zoe and Terry are retired now. Or you could think of it as an area of extremely high unemployment. Lots of dinners, parties, even a rock star performed. Well, he was an Elvis impersonator of excellent ability.

And then one day the world stopped. Planes no longer flew overhead. We are not far from DFW airport. Although our neighborhood is many miles away from the events on 9/11 we sat in our homes and watched TV with heavy hearts and prayed for our fellow citizens and country. The next day we lined the cul de sac with little three-inch American Flags—they were the biggest we could find. On Friday night President Bush requested that the country has an evening of prayer. So everybody living on our cul de sac gathered in the back yard. We held hands, we lit candles, we sang Good Bless America and Colleen led us in a prayer. I was pretty sure America was united on that evening. I know the cul de sac was. A little later we put a flag pole on the highest hill of the cul de sac as our way of remembering.

CARL AND JAYNNE

If we thought it was a miracle that Larry got married at 35, imagine our surprise that Carl and Jaynne got married at 38. He an MD, she a PHD. Well the whole town of Abilene was surprised. That's why 800 people turned out for the wedding. And there they were, at the front of the church; Carl and his brother Ray with their 1000-megawatt smiles. Everybody said I do, and they did. I guess Carl and Jaynne were too busy with their careers to get started any earlier. Several years before their marriage he even threatened to take her out, but he let seven years go by before he did. It is probably a good thing; she might have turned him down.

Now I can tell you a lot about Carl and Jaynne. For example, their tattoos, but I won't. The romance and love story aside, their marriage was more like a merger of two pack rats and three cats. It is a true image to conjure. But I am getting ahead of the story.

Abilene, Texas, is a good example of the term "wrong side of the tracks." The tracks run down the middle of town and divide the city by north and south. Even the street names are north and south. On the north side of town the homes are older and smaller. On the south side the homes are newer and bigger. My grandmother Bessie and her kids grew up and lived on the north side of town.

The first house that I remember Carl's mother having was on the north side of town, not too far from Bessie. Now there is nothing wrong with the people on the north side of town. Generally speaking, they just had less money than those on the other side of the tracks.

Carl spent most of his youth growing up on the south side of town, but they were not in one of the large fancy houses. Carl and his brother Ray grew up in the Hendrick Home for Children. Carl's father was an officer in the military, but he liked drinking more than anything else.

Unlike Charles, he didn't quit. In the early 50's, Carl's mother Barbara, like Jim McCormick, was attacked by polio. There was no one to take care of Carl and his younger brother.

The Hendrick Home for Children was founded in 1939 by West Texas pioneers Thomas and Ida Hendrick after their only child, Four-year-old Joseph died. They established the home and dedicated their lives and resources to serve children on a long-term basis. The Home is still meeting needs of kids today. There are hundreds of success stories. Carl's is only one of many. The Hendrick Home paid for Carl and Ray to go to college and then medical school for Carl. Ray became a Pharmacist. Carl and Ray both returned to Abilene to serve the community that served them so well.

The first time I met Carl we were both 18-year-old freshmen at Hardin-Simmons University. He was sitting at a table drinking coffee and all the people at the table were talking about baseball. Carl was offering his opinion. The subject changed to opera and Carl had an opinion about this, too. I had never met anyone before who knew about opera. And he knew about baseball. I knew right then this was a smart guy. So, when he married an opera singer instead of a baseball player, I was not surprised.

I wanted Carl as a friend. I wanted to hang out with smart people. This is something I have tried to do all my life. I keep hoping some of it might rub off on me. Carl and I became room—mates our junior year and Ray moved in our senior year.

Over the years I have had a front row seat to his remarkable life. After medical school, Carl became a flight surgeon in the navy. He could fly the jets. He spent a year in Antarctica as the naval base doctor there. He had a tour of the Pacific and Atlantic oceans. When he got out of the navy, he opened his medical practice in Abilene. I could say he became a prominent physician, but he probably wouldn't like that. In 2005 he was selected by Hardin-Simmons University as one of its Distinguished Alumni.

One of the first things Carl did when he returned home was to buy his mother a beautiful new home, on the south side of Abilene. I do not know if Barbara made a deal with God the way Jim McCormick did, but she had a long career as the receptionist at the West Texas Rehabilitation Center. In fact, the reception room at the Center is named in her honor. Carl and Jaynne probably would not like for me to mention that they give a lot of money to charities in Abilene, so I won't.

On a cold winter night, not too long after Carl and Jaynne were married, Ray was driving home from Lubbock to Abilene. He must have misjudged the ice. He died in a one-car accident. He had married his high school sweetheart and left behind his wife and two lovely daughters.

Today, Carl and Jaynne live in a house on the south side of Abilene, but just barely. It is in the historic area where the homes are almost a hundred years old. Their home is a craftsman style home. Sometimes houses suit their people. This one does. Remember, earlier I said they were kind of like two pack rats that moved in together; well they have not changed their ways.

We see Carl and Jaynne a lot. Zoe and the two of them, together with our friend Jim, have season tickets to the Dallas Opera. Let me also add that when Carl and Jaynne make a trip to the Dallas area, it is very good for the local economy. Jaynne calls it "retail therapy." And one more thing, I mean what the hell … his is a penguin and hers is a cat paw. But I am not going to tell you where they are.

KIRBY,LYDA, AND BOONE

Kirby is ten years younger than me. When he started working for me at the American Heart Association, I told him I thought he was a natural-born salesman. It turns out I was right. This is how my business career happened.

I was at a cocktail party for some event. Lyda Hill was talking to me. She says "Terry, if you are ever going to make any money, you are going to have to get out of charity work." This might seem strange to some, because at the time of this conversation, I was getting paid for my charity work. Lyda was doing it for free.

Lyda is one of the most interesting people I have ever known, and at this point, I hope you think I have known some pretty interesting people. The first time I met her she, was barefoot in her downtown office. She was busy at the time running her travel business, being Chairman of the Crystal Charity Ball, and making time to talk to me about what I wanted her to do for the American Heart Association. I don't think she was thirty yet. When she sold the travel business, it was one of the largest travel agencies in Dallas, if not the country. While Lyda had some family connections, she did not use them to start her business.

The Crystal Charity Ball netted over $500,000 that year, a staggering amount of money for a ball, at the time. She did help the American Heart Association and many other charities. She told her family she worked 50% on business projects and 60% on charity projects. She worked a lot, and she was very good at both. She still is. I hope she writes her memoirs someday.

A few days after my conversation with Lyda, I was in Houston at a meeting with Jere Mitchell MD. He is head of Cardiovascular Research at UT Medical School in Dallas. Also in this meeting was T. Boone Pickens of Amarillo. Boone was on the fast track to becoming a

Texas Legend. At this time, he was only a semi—legend. When the meeting was over, Boone asked Dr. Mitchell and I if we wanted a lift back to Dallas. We told him we had reservations on Southwest Airlines. He says "Save the money. I will get you there faster anyway."

This is how I ended up on the private jet of T. Boone Pickens. Later the media drops the T. But I noticed the life style Mr. Pickens was living. It was my only time to ride on a private plane.

Later that afternoon, I am sitting on my deck in the heart of Oak Lawn in Dallas having some Jack Daniels. I am thinking, "You know, when the granddaughter of H.L. Hunt tells you to get out of charity and you get a ride with Boone Pickens on a private plane, maybe you should look for a different job." The next day I do.

Twenty five years went by pretty damn quick. I did some things right, and some wrong. You will learn about those in a bit. I learned a lot. I do not regret working for the charities, because I believe it kept me from developing "greedy bastard syndrome." That disease, left untreated, will ruin you and the business. Of course, early on I call Kirby and say, "It's time for you to be a salesman." He agrees.

I always thought Kirby looked like a younger, trimmer version of Tom Selleck. One day we were in downtown Dallas for a meeting. After the meeting we go to a parking garage to get our car. I go over to the waiting area, and Kirby goes to pay the cashier. In the waiting area next to me are two attractive women dressed like lawyers. One says to the other, "Wow, he is just drop-your-pants gorgeous!" When I realized they were not talking about me, I also realized that I didn't know women talked that way.

The business that we are in helps companies improve their hiring process. As a result, it can save companies considerable costs. The brain behind the technical side of our business is Chuck. He tells me one day that he believes our process will work, but he adds, "I don't know why anyone would pay us for it." So I tell him, "We will just have to sit down and make up some reasons, and then Kirby and I will go sell people on the concept." So that afternoon we make up some reasons, and the next day Kirby and I start selling.

What we were really doing was debate class 101. Maridell Fryar taught me this when I was eighteen. It is need, plan, plan meets need, and then convince them you are right. In this case, the service we offered was what the companies needed. We had to show our clients we could provide the service and give them cost benefit back in return. We did, it works. Hundreds of the largest companies in America use the service.

Kirby tells me later, "You know the best sale you ever made was convincing me it would work." One day more than fifteen years ago, Kirby was on a sales trip to Chicago. He signs up one of the largest, most well known, and most admired companies in the country. But when the deal is almost closed, the head guy says, "But of course we will have to run it by legal." Legal turns out to be Jodi. Well, he not only runs it by her, he grabs her and hauls her butt off to the altar. Or maybe she did the grabbing and hauling. I am not sure. They have been married ever since. And I have racked my brains for years trying to remember what that lawyer type woman in the parking garage looked like.

ODDS AND ENDS

Kirby got a chance to read a first draft of the first part of these memoirs. He says to me, "I notice you didn't mention your first wife." I say "Not yet, and I don't plan on mentioning yours either."

The baby boomer generation has many things attributed to it. One is a higher divorce rate than previous generations. I think that is because we don't see any harm or foul in a false start. It was just a false start. Do it right the next time. A false start in football is when a player moves too early. In marriage, it's when two people move too early. In football, a five-yard penalty is imposed. If it's early in the game, it usually doesn't cost you much. But late in the game it can be a different matter. In my case, it was early in the game. The penalty was the $300 stereo I happily carried to her daddy's pick up. It was the only asset we had accumulated in the few months of the false start.

Do you remember earlier I mentioned that Grady Paul and I had qualified for the National Debate Tournament? We did not get to go because Grady Paul was on scholastic probation, and the university president said no. Well it happens that Grady Paul gets back at him, with the president's worst nightmare. A false start with his daughter.

False starts are also when you get up in the morning and realize you were over served the previous evening, so you go back to bed. Hence, a false start.

Carl and Jaynne have offered up a corollary to the false start. The cat sucked on my hair. If you had too much adult beverage one evening and get up the next day with hair awry and head of ache, then the cat sucked on your hair. It is the only rational explanation. This easily explains why I have so little hair.

The year after Carl and Jaynne are married, we go on a vacation with them to South Padre Island. This is the Texas Rivera. While we are there, we also go across the border to the town of Matamoros. It is here that Zoe and Jaynne discover an upscale clothing shop called Barbara's. Barbara knows a trick or two. She offers "free Margaritas" to her customers. Well, I guess the average price of those drinks was about $200 each. Loaded with treasures, they join Carl and me at the Las Dos Republicas' bar, where the margaritas are not free, but are much cheaper.

After a few rounds we head back to the Island for dinner at Scampi's. This is a very nice, most excellent restaurant. Of course, Zoe and Jaynne split a couple bottles of wine. You should know that Carl and I have reserved a deep sea fishing charter for 7AM the next morning, so we are pacing ourselves. The ladies were enjoying. But overnight the cat sucked on their hair.

The next morning we all go to the boat and take off. One way to fish off shore is to slowly troll through the sea with lures. Sometimes you also use some stuff called "chum." This is basically a bucket of fish parts. Looks like cold gumbo. The idea is that as you throw out the chum, fish are attracted to the area and then you slowly drag your lure through the chum.

We did not have any chum. But we did have Jaynne and Zoe. It seems a combination of libations, dinner and breakfast, along with a gently rolling ocean, brought up all of the chum we needed. If you have an image in your mind, where Carl and I are holding our wives feet, while the rest of their body dangles over the back of the boat puking, then you are pretty close.

Immediately Carl and I started catching fish, King Mackerels about thirty pounds each. We caught so many and got so tired we didn't have time to drink the beer or eat the snicker bars we brought. Carl and I were quick to credit Zoe and Jaynne's contribution to the fishing trip, but they were lying on the floor of the boat. I am not sure they heard us.

I mentioned that Zoe and I have lots of dinner parties. One of the things I like to do (if I am still awake) is to ask a question of the group. I do this because I want everyone present to be able to tell a story. The stories are always better than the question. One night, our friends Jim and Kenny are in attendance. My question to the group is, "Tell us about your first car." Kenny quickly adds, "And did you have sex in it." It made for more interesting answers.

When I grew up in Midland we would go to Grandmother Bessie's house for Thanksgiving. We had all the usual trimmings; I especially remember the fruit salad. But, there was a difference of opinion about cornbread dressing. I have seen this on other occasions when there is more than one good cook present. My grandmother knew she was a good cook. My mother knew she was a good cook. But the question was, "do you use yellow corn meal to make dressing or white corn meal."

You see when Mother used white corn meal, Mom Maw said, "It's just not as good." When yellow was used, Bessie was happy. One Thanksgiving the dressing was yellow. Bessie smiled, until mother pulled out the white corn meal and yellow food dye. I learned a valuable lesson that day from my mother. Never fool your mother!

THE POLTICS OF MARRIAGE

It occurs to me that three couples on the cul de sac have over a hundred years of marriage among them. And that does not even count the false starts. We also have some friends that are married, and they are gay. Now the governments of Texas and America don't recognize this marriage, but most of us on the cul de sac do.

Of course I remind myself that these are the same governments that thought it was okay to kill Indians and then put the survivors on reservations. The same governments that thought it was okay to enslave black people. And the same governments that thought it was okay to deny women the right to vote.

I understand why some churches don't want to recognize gay marriage. I think that is just fine for a church. But it is not fine for our government. This is the land of the free and home of the brave. I guess we are not that brave to be that free. Dick Cheney was right. Freedom means freedom for everybody. Human beings should be able to marry a human being of their choice. The government's role is to provide for equal rights under the law. The government's job is not to decide who marries who.

LITTLE BROTHER

The first time I met Michael was in November of 1949. The first recollection I have of him was when I started the first grade. I would come home and tell Mother everything I had done during the day, and, of course, all of the new kids I was meeting. After a few days of this, Michael starts telling us of his day and his friends. One of his friends was Murmur; I don't remember the other two. These, of course, were imaginary friends. Now today that kid would be in therapy and on some drug to cure him. Our mother just figured he was reacting to me starting school and meeting new people and he would just outgrow it. Far as I know, he did. I think that mothers were smarter in those days.

When I was about eleven or twelve, and Michael was about eight, Mother decided we should take piano lessons from Kenneth Newsome. I spent six months learning how to play "Swiss Lullaby," the only song I learned how to play. After I played the song at a recital, Mother agreed to let me quit piano and play football. But Michael is different. He learned how to play lots of songs. He learned how to write them, arrange them, and sing them. He is pretty good. He also learned how to play the guitar. And in high school he learned how to play the cornet and joined the band.

His freshman year at high school was my freshman year at college. His first day of school at Midland Lee went like this. As a member of the band, he had to be at school early since band practice was scheduled before school started. That morning he bent over to help put up some instruments and the entire seat of his pants rip from top to bottom. He doesn't know a what, or a who, or a where. But he remembers about me talking about Maridell Fryar, the debate coach. Her classroom is across the hall from the band area.

He walks over and sees her. He goes in and says, "I know you don't know me, but my brother is Terry, and look what has happened to my pants. What I can do?" Well, she goes for her purse and pulls out her car keys, points out her car, and says "Go home and change." So he does. You are right, he was fourteen, never driven a car before. Today she would probably be arrested. But everything turned out just fine.

An older brother can be a problem for a younger brother, especially if he is held to some high standard that people think the older brother set. This is where I do my brother a huge favor. When Michael gets to high school, no one is going to hold him to a high standard. I remember sitting in Ms. Bellomy's English class and hearing her booming voice say, "Smart people know words." Hey, I was on the debate team, I knew words. But there is a catch; these English teachers want you to be able to spell them.

My freshman year in college, Mrs. Mathis says to me in front of the whole class, "Mr. Broxson, you will never amount to a thing because you cannot spell." I reply, "Doesn't matter, my secretary will." My spelling and smartass remarks got me an "F" and I had to retake the class. But I was right about the secretary.

Michael's best friend growing up was Big John. They were the same age and met at the Baptist church. Big John had a brother a couple years older than me. Big John was a regular at the church; his brother was a semi-regular. When I turned fourteen, I moved up to the older kids' class for Sunday School and Training Union. Training Union was the evening Sunday School.

One evening I am in class with Big John's brother. The lady who is the teacher this night gets on a roll. She has three teen-aged daughters in the class. The teacher says, "What would the world be like if everyone acted like you?" She must have really liked this, because she repeated it louder. "What would the world be like if everyone acted like you?" Well, Big John's brother dressed in jeans, white shirt and leather jacket, a lot like Fonzie, says, "Well, it would probably be over-populated." Silence. Laughter. First from the daughters. Then the mother. I am thinking these are going to be more educational classes.

But you know the best thing about the classes at the Baptist Church … there was no spelling test.

Big John lived large, maybe that's why he was called Big John. One day he is flying his ultra light air craft. The bracing on the wing fails. The little plane falls to the West Texas plains. He was thirty-two.

Today, Michael lives alone in a log house under tall pine trees. He doesn't want a pickle, but he likes to ride his motorcycle. His hair is white; he didn't have a cat to suck his out like me. His beard makes him look like a slim Santa. He has had a couple of false starts. The first one gave him a son, and a granddaughter. The second one gave him a daughter, and a granddaughter and a grandson.

Remember the central character in the story called Flower Power? Her name is Lou Ann. Turns out she has also had a couple of false starts, and she has a son (a Marine no less) and a daughter who is planning on being a doctor. So you can see where I am going with this. Lou Ann lives on Nob Hill in San Francisco. Maybe we can get Tom Hanks to star as Michael, and Meg Ryan can star as Lou Ann. We could call the movie "Senseless in East Texas." She could sing the instrumentals and he could play them. That part is fiction, but wouldn't it be a great way to end a book.

COMPETITION

I don't know what makes people competitive I just know I am. What ever the project I want to do it right and I want to win. When I was eleven, my father taught me how to bowl. There were a lot of people who bowled in Midland. My father was one of the top ten in town. By the time I was fifteen I was one of the top three. I am being modest only Bob McGregor was better. Bob was a few years older and he became a professional. I could have.

When I was sixteen I was bowling in men's leagues and averaging 210. But the real action came later after leagues were over, pot games. Gambling. Any where from five to twenty people would bet various amounts in some form of competition. My father played in these and won his fair share.

One day a man from Odessa, JD, a rich oil man who liked to bowl, approached my father about me. He said he would like to team me up with a twenty-three year old fellow from Odessa and see if we could make some money. J.D. said he would pay expenses and put up the gambling money and then give my father half of what we won. My father could settle with me. I think I was getting two dollars a week allowance.

That summer I was sixteen. We traveled all over west Texas, and we won a lot. It was not unusual for these games to go late into the night or early in the morning. All of the people we competed against were older twenties, thirties, and up. These older guys were usually drinking. They couldn't beat me sober. They had no business drinking and then gambling against me. But they did. I remember times some of their wives would try to talk the men out of the game. But they rarely succeeded. I must admit this bothered me, maybe because of the Baptist Church.

When that summer was over I started my junior year in high school, I told my father I was quitting bowling. He said that was fine it was up to me. This is when I joined the debate team and found that using the brain for competition was more fun and harder than throwing a 16 pound bowling ball down an alley.

Competition also came in handy when Kirby and I got to the business of selling. Kirby learned his skills at the country club playing golf. He is still pretty good. We would compete for who made the most sells. Now I will tell you the truth. I did not mind losing this competition. If he won I still won. He would compete with me at bowling, poker, gin rummy, and almost any thing. One time we are on vacation fishing. He says "I am going to catch more fish than you." I say "Kirby, we are on vacation we are here to relax." He says "Oh, ok I am going to relax more than you."

AUTOMOBILES

I guess every generation since the dang things were invented has had a love affair with the automobile. I know the baby boomers have. I also think the cars of the 50's and 60's are among the coolest cars ever built. My first car was a 1955 pea green Chevy. I was sixteen. And no Kenny, I did not have sex in it. I don't think a girl ever rode in it. I know that when church services on Sunday nights were over; I rode in someone else's car. You did not want to be the driver for Pudunkel and Pudiddle.

The first new car I remember my Dad buying was a 1956 black and red Buick Road Master—what a great car. The first new car I ever bought was a 1972 Ford Pinto. A piece of crap, but I really loved it. The first new car Zoe and I got was a 1975 Chrysler Cordova. It was red, and even though Ricardo Montalban advertised that it was available in Corinthian Leather, ours had a cloth interior that was called Indian Blanket. My friend Phil gets in it and says, "Damn, This is like being in a Navajo whorehouse." I did defer all knowledge of Navajo whorehouses to Phil.

Grady Paul drove a 1953 Plymouth through out high school and college that he called Ben. This was short for Ben's full name, Been Getting Any. A most favorite greeting of Grady Paul's was to call out to someone "Terry, been getting any?" "Any what Grady Paul?" "Taller," he replied.

Zoe has, and will forever want to have, a convertible. So in 1976 I bought a 1968 MGB, a little two-seat roadster convertible. One thing I had never learned to do was work on cars. I paid $1500 for this car, and decided since I was a college graduate; surely I could work on cars and restore this worn-out junk heap to pristine working condition. I went to the auto store and bought a Chilton Manuel for MGB's. This was the complete guide to repairs for this vehicle. The first thing that needed repaired was the clutch. So I open up my manual to find the chapter on clutch repair. "Step One … Remove Engine." What the hell kind of step one is that? I thought maybe, "Take a crescent wrench and remove bolt on left." After about $1000 of repairs, I sold it to a dentist for $1300. I have never bought a used car since, or a Chilton Manual. Nor did I ever try to be that dentist's patient.

My first recollection of riding in an automobile was one Saturday morning, in 1954, when mother roused Michael and me out of bed about 5 AM. We were going to Abilene for a visit with grandmother Bessie. Since it was so early and still dark, my little brother was laid on pillows on the passenger side with a blanket and went to sleep. I was placed in the back seat with pillows and a blanket. That's probably what saved our lives.

Just outside of Stanton on Highway 80, a two-lane highway before the interstates were built, a man driving west fell asleep and crossed into Mother's lane as we headed east. I will never forget my mother's cries for help. She was trapped in the wreckage. Michael had banged his head when he was tossed into the dashboard. I was thrown into the seat cushions, not a scratch. Mother had a concussion, broken nose, broken arm and ankles. In the other car the daughter survived. Her parents were not as lucky.

BEN DENMAN

I met Ben when he was sixty-eight years old. He was a very good friend of Jim McCormick. At sixty-five Ben retired as President of Southwestern Life Insurance Company. At the time I believe it was the largest insurance company in Dallas. Ben told me when he retired; he had to have heart bypass surgery. He also said he had to quit smoking. I guess it worked. A few months ago I wished him a happy ninetieth birthday. Jim and Ben became instrumental in helping me and my partners achieve our success. They had their own office with us, advisors, supporters, and friends.

Ben graduated from the University of Texas in 1942. He joined the Navy and requested service in the Pacific. He had a personal mission. Ben had married Nell Dyess. She was the daughter of a County Judge from Albany Texas. Her brother was Edwin Dyess, a lieutenant colonel in the Army Air Corps. Col. Dyess was in the Philippines when Pearl Harbor was attacked. He led a small group of pilots against an enemy that vastly outnumbered and outgunned them. He and his men were captured and went on the infamous Bataan Death March. He survived. A year later he escaped.

Officially, Col. Dyess made his way back to Washington and briefed the War Department. Ben told me he also briefed Roosevelt. Roosevelt said the complete story of the Death March could not yet be told. The American people would have been outraged, and would have demanded action. But the war effort was not in a position to respond. Col. Dyess was going to return to action. In the process he was in Southern California flying a P 38 when it caught fire over a highly populated area. He stayed with the plane and crashed in a vacant lot, giving his life to his country. Ben told me there was no proof, but sabotage was suspected. Dyess Air Force base in Abilene is named after him.

Ben and Nell moved to Lake Jackson a few years ago to be closer to their son. They left Dallas a far better place than they found it. Ben was a volunteer with countless hours of charity work. He told me he preferred to be an Indian, not a Chief. Nell is one of the primary reasons Dallas has the Arboretum and Botanical Gardens.

CAREER PATHS

My first paying job was at Shamrock Lanes bowling alley, when I was twelve. I rented bowling shoes to people. I made 50 cents an hour. I did this off and on for four years. When I was nineteen, home from college in the summer, I worked in the oil fields on a survey crew, mostly cutting mesquite brush. I made $12 per day. In college I worked as a delivery boy for Shaw's office supply. I worked four hours a day and made 90 cents an hour.

When I graduated college in May of 1968, I tried to join the Navy. This seemed like the best choice, because I was going to be drafted. I figured I would have a better chance of surviving Viet Nam on a ship than on the ground. But, I flunked the physical. The doctors thought I might be diabetic. When I was drafted and retested, the Army said I was 4F, not fit to serve. At 6' 3" and 225 Pounds, I didn't look 4F. So I did the only reasonable thing and got into the University of Texas Law School. My father made it clear to me. He said if I wanted to be a lawyer that was fine with him. Although, he said he personally didn't have much use for them. But he had my brother starting college, and I would have to pay for Law School. He took me down to the Midland National Bank and they loaned me $1000 for the first semester, but only because my father co signed the note.

I learned a lot in Law School. But the thing I learned the most is that I didn't want to go to school any more. Faced with two and half more years of school, and several thousand dollars of debt, I decided to cut losses, get a job, and pay off the $1000. So I did.

Burroughs Corporation offered me $500 a month to go Beaumont and become a salesman. This is interesting only in hindsight, because if I had taken that job, there is a good chance I would have met Zoe earlier because she worked at a bank in Beaumont. She tells me now that Burroughs's salesmen were always coming by. But the American Cancer

Society offered me $525 a month to go to Waco. There was also the "hippy factor." Working for a charity was better than working for a big company. But from my perspective—$25 was $25. Hello Waco.

AMERICAN CANCER SOCIETY

My job was to help organize and support volunteers in about seventeen central Texas countries that carried out the business of the American Cancer Society. There were lots of activities. But let's be honest. The chief activity was raising money. My boss was Jack Hardison. He told me from the first interview that if the volunteers are successful then you are successful. Get things done through other people. That was a good lesson. I have used it lot.

I also had a company car. My first one was a stripped down no frills 1968 Plymouth, but it had 363 horses under the hood. My typical day started before 8 AM, and usually three or four nights a week I had a meeting in various towns around Waco. These meetings might last till 9 or 10PM. I could be as far away as ninety miles. But I would be home in an hour. That Plymouth could almost fly. I put 38,000 miles on the car the first year, just driving around central Texas. I knew the roads really well.

The first year the volunteers were very successful. Mr. Curt Reiman presented me with an award for most improved fund raising at the annual staff conference. In presenting me the award, he said. "If the world ever got an enema it would go up the main street of Waco." I did not agree of his assessment of Waco. But him being the big boss and all I took the award, and kept my mouth shut. Something I would not always do.

Curt was the very charismatic Head Honcho of the Staff of the Texas American Cancer Society. He was a decorated officer in World War II. He probably did more than any single individual to bring effective management that streamlined and improved how most health agencies operate in this country. He had a protégée, Dudley Hafner, who would go on to lead the American Heart Association, in Texas and nationally. These were two of the most brilliant men I have ever known. They could have run General Motors or IBM. Our state and country are better off because they didn't. I was fortunate to work for both of them. Remember; get around smart people, sometimes it rubs off.

The second year I am in Waco the volunteers do very well again. I am offered a promotion to move to Dallas and be the Assistant Executive Director in charge of fund raising. I know this is the plum job in the country, because Dallas was one of the largest best-run offices and the volunteers were very successful. I get a $1000 a year raise. A few months earlier, for reasons I can no longer remember, I had married a girl from Waco. But it seems that she prefers to stay in Waco with her mother than move to Dallas. So hence, my false start.

In this job, I am a 24-year-old kid surround by tall buildings and taller people. I don't know where else a young person could work with the likes of a Bill Zale, co founder of the Zale Corporation, Herman Lay, founder of Lays Potato Chips and Chairman of Frito Lay, and a whole lot of others.

Mr. Zale was the first Fund Raising Chairman I worked with. The fund raising drive in those days was about a month long. It was highly organized into divisions. Such as: residential door to door, accountants, lawyers, special gifts (higher dollar types), employee drives for large employers, Cancer Control Day (a day where hundreds of life insurance agents would solicit small business for a donation), as well as others. It was a massive organization. It was my job to see that it worked.

While the funds drive was only a month long, it took months of work to recruit all the volunteers and organize all the records and materials that were necessary to be successful. This job I had for two years was called the meat grinder. Here's why. I started my day usually about 7:30 AM. Mr. Zale would call me every morning about 8:15 and say,

"Terry, how did we do yesterday" and I would tell him. For about ten months I worked until 10PM. I worked almost every Saturday and some Sundays.

Since volunteers did the fund raising, my job was to keep track of who was doing well, and who wasn't. Some times I had to tell Mr. Zale who had not performed. Mr. Zale would say, "Give me their phone number." In those days no businessman in Dallas wanted to get a phone call from Bill Zale asking why they had not finished their assignment. This was a power I had. I learned that I needed to know what was going on before I told Mr. Zale. I only informed him of problems I couldn't fix. I didn't have any clout or juice. He did. But I got to ride his coattails.

Here is one quick story about Herman Lay, the founder of Lay's Potato Chips. I have read that he started the business as a young man, maybe ten at the time. I believe he lived in Georgia. He would make his chips up at home and then walk to town to sell them. When I met him, he was probably in his sixties. After a meeting one evening we are walking out of the building, and he says "Terry, come over to my car. I want to give you something." He opens up the trunk and hands me two bags of potato chips, and says, "These are brand new, and they are great!" He really liked his business.

After two years in the meat grinder, I quit. I work in the insurance business for about 3 months, but I don't like this much. So when the people at the Cystic Fibrosis Foundation offer the job of Executive Director in Houston. I take it. And then, I met Doris Day. But you already knew that.

AMERICAN HEART ASSOCIATION

Dudley was the big boss, Cass was number 2. They offered me the opportunity to be the Executive Director in Dallas. They said they wanted new management. They got it. Dudley looked out at the staff one time at a conference and said, "This group sure works hard and they play harder." He may have been referring to the time my buddy Sam and I went to a Staff conference at MO Ranch, a meeting facility outside of Kerrville.

It's about a six hour drive from Dallas. Sam who was newly hired in the Ft. Worth office had also worked for the American Cancer Society. He offers to pick me up about 10:30 in the morning as we will drive down together. We put a cooler with a case of beer in the car for the trip. Children don't try this at home. When we get to Austin, after driving three hours, we stop and get another case of beer. When we get to MO ranch, we were out of beer, brains, and the meeting starts in twenty minutes. Sam and I were the new breed, the new management that Dudley and Cass wanted. We must have been impressive. We could tell this, because we still had a job the next day. There is an old saying about being careful for what you wish for, because you might get it.

I worked for the AHA for almost eight years. I had the opportunity to know some wonderful people; some were on the staff and many others who volunteered their time. Here are a few of the stories that live in these decaying brain cells.

I was at a meeting in San Antonio. It is a nice luxury retreat. A young couple checks into the hotel. They are newlyweds. Next to them is Mike Skiles, our executive in Ft. Worth. Sam had moved on to Houston. As the check in proceeds, Mike takes notice of their room number. A few minutes after they get in the room, their phone rings, the young bride says, "Hello".

"Hello madam, my name is the Reverend Skiles. I work as part of a service of this fine hotel. I want you to know I am on duty should you have any questions during your stay."

A little laughter from the bride.

"Now we know that newlyweds can have questions, so do you have any questions at this time?"

More laughter, she says, "NO".

He says, "Well, if you do, please free to call the front desk and ask for the reverend." For ever more he was the Reverend Skiles.

Lyda Hill was the first woman elected Chairman of the Board of the Dallas Heart Association. Feminist rights were a hot topic of the day. I ask Lyda if she prefers to be called Chairwoman of the Board. She says, "No the title is a position not a gender." Besides she says that she is Miss not a Ms., and proud of it. That year she also played in the charity golf tournament that benefited the Heart Association. She was the only woman who played. No, she didn't win, but she did win the longest driving competition. She beat some members of the Dallas Cowboys.

One of the things I did right was to suggest to the committee that nominates the officers and directors of the Heart Association that Jere Mitchell, MD be considered as President of the Association. Dr. Mitchell was the Chief of Cardiovascular research at the University of Texas Southwestern Medical School in Dallas. Up to this point, the only presidents of the Heart Association were physicians in private practice. The doctors on the committee thought this was a great idea. Since the Heart Association funded research, it was always thought that the research physicians had a vested interest and might somehow corrupt the system. But this was not the case. Here is an example.

When Dr. Mitchell became President, he told me he wanted to bring a couple of the young physician researchers to a board meeting so that community members could hear about some of the medical research that was going on locally. I said, "Well, Jere, do you think that might be a little technical and over everybody's head?" He says, "Maybe, but I think they should understand why they are raising money and what it is going for." This how I first met and heard two young guys named Drs. Joe Goldstein and Michael Brown. They met with about thirty members of the Board of Directors, and told us our first news about the effects of cholesterol and triglycerides and heart disease. Dr. Mitchell knew these two fellows were doing outstanding work. The rest of the world would find out a few years later, when they were presented the Nobel Prize for Medicine.

Dr. Mitchell is truly one of the good guys of life. When I first met him, he was the spitting image of John Denver. Jere is an East Texas boy who grew up in Longview. He also introduced me to another friend of his Stanley Marcus. At the time, he was Chairman Emeritus of Neiman Marcus. The meeting was at Mr. Marcus's downtown office. Whenever anyone thinks of Stanley Marcus, you would have to think of style and class. In person, he did not disappoint. Everything from his office to his secretary to the small china cups we drank coffee from were first cabin. Dr. Mitchell explained to Mr. Marcus the role the American Heart Association had in providing some initial seed money for medical research. He said, "Stanley, the problem is that the federal government provides the vast majority of the research funds, but they are like a pendulum that swings from year to year, and it's hard to know how your funding will be on a yearly basis." Mr. Marcus laughed, and said, "Well Jere, in this country we call that pendulum swinging democracy and it is preferable to communism where the pendulum does not swing."

Roger Horchow was another friend of Dr. Mitchell. He was a protégé of Stanley Marcus. He worked for Neiman Marcus as a buyer and traveled all over world looking for unique things. He found a lot of them. He left Neiman Marcus and founded the Horchow Collection, a fabulous catalog and very successful business. Of all the people I have known and worked with Roger Horchow intimidated me the most. He had the most piercing stare when he would look at you over his reading glasses. He'd ask hard questions, and I was never sure I was answering them right.

When I left the American Heart Association, Dr. Mitchell gave a farewell dinner party for Zoe and me at his house. A wonderful evening I will always remember. On my last day at work, I received one letter from a volunteer thanking me for the work I had done in Dallas. The letter was from Roger Horchow. Imagine my delight a few years later seeing him on television receiving the Tony Award for Producer of the best Musical on Broadway, "Crazy About You."

THE BACK BUSINESS

I left the Heart Association and went to work for two entrepreneur physicians named Stephen Hochschuler and Ralph Rashbaum. These are highly intelligent, gifted men. Steve also has a very sharp sense of humor. He told me that he advised his buddy in high school to give up this singing gig because he just wasn't any good. It was Art Garfunkel. Ralph and Steve have had great success in a variety of projects. I wish I could say I was one of them, but I wasn't.

The first three years I was the Executive Vice President of the North Texas Back Institute. This was an out patient rehabilitation facility for people suffering from back pain. I think my work during this period was at least adequate to maybe above average. The real job Steve and Ralph wanted me to do was to figure out how to develop other businesses that were related.

THE BACK PLACE

We got the idea from an article in the Wall Street Journal, about a guy in Boston who had opened up a retail place for items just for people who had back problems. I fly up to Boston and go in and buy a few things, got to talk to the owner and ask a bunch of questions. I report back. We envisioned that we can do this, too, and probably better. We thought we could open up a chain of these stores across the country.

What we needed was a business model that worked. We needed someone to manage it, and we need working capital and some expertise. This is where I met Jim McCormick, an investment banker with a track record of success. Stanley Pearle joined the group. He had founded Pearle Vision. Lee Trevino joined as an investor and spokesperson and several others. We raised $500,000. We hired Leland to run it.

We opened two stores with great fanfare. Leland was extremely capable and worked very hard, but sales at the store simply never got to a break even point. We ran out of money and closed. It was just that simple. The investors lost their money, took a tax write off, and went on down the road. Leland and I thought that our problem was that we had not raised enough money to begin with. If that was right, we were not the first company to be under funded. This fact might be true because today, almost twenty years later, there are stores all across the country that do exactly what we were trying to do. The last time I saw Leland, he was running some of them. Good for him.

BACK SYSTEMS, INC

When you surround yourself with smart people and surround yourself with their money, it seems it would be impossible to fail. Well, you can. Particularly, when you get a little help from the Federal government. This is a true story of how I lost some good people's money that I really did not want to lose.

The idea was that we could start a company that that would provide services to large corporations to manage their cost of medical back injuries. We had three ideas of service. First, we would work with insurance companies to manage the cost of the claim. Another would provide training and design services to make the workplace safer. The third would help companies match job applicants with the physical demands of the job.

Jim McCormick was instrumental in putting together the group of investors. I did my friend Lyda Hill the favor of getting her to join the group. With friends like me she didn't need enemies. There were several other investors as well.

The chief investor was a real estate tycoon named Craig Hall. When Jim introduced me to Craig he was thirty-four years old and the newspapers were saying he was already worth over $250 million, a very tidy sum for 1984. Jim would tell me that he thought one day Craig might be the richest man on the planet because he was smart, driven and young. I sure didn't help him. I wished I could have.

The company was funded with $300,000 from the investors including Craig. I even borrowed $10,000 from the bank to put in the kitty. Craig also provided a line of credit to the company in the amount of one million dollars. Craig's investment was not a personal check, but rather through a company he owned a savings and loan.

I had a new title after my name. President, Back Systems, Inc.

We got right to work and we could sell our services. But what we could not do is make a profit. The problem was that providing the service was too labor intensive. We were trying to develop computer systems that would allow us to leverage our efficacy, but we were running out of money. So we made a decision to concentrate on the physical ability testing part of the business that Chuck was developing. This decision meant that a lot of good people lost their jobs. It also reduced our overhead.

We were able to convince seven large food distribution companies to fund a study to validate that our physical ability testing would meet the federal guidelines for hiring decisions. This contract, along with our line of credit from Craig meant that we could probably survive for the year and half this study would take. If the study proved what we all thought it would, then a business model would be possible.

But this is what happened. In the late 80's real estate and the saving and loan industry was in turmoil and failing badly. The federal government would take over the S&L industry and put some bad guys in jail. Craig Hall was not one of the bad guys. When all things were crashing around him, we wondered if the last $100,000 on the line of credit would be available to us. Craig met with me, Jim, and Ben and said, "I live up to my commitments." He did.

But the FDIC took over Craig's Savings and Loan Company. Jim, Ben, and I are called in for a meeting with the FDIC people. They wanted to know what our prospects were for paying back the one million dollar loan. We told them that we were almost finished with this study that would validate our business model for physical ability testing. They took maybe three minutes trying to understand our business, but quickly gave up.

As I recall there were three young lawyer types in the meeting. They ask us how much money we had in the bank, and what assets we had that we could sell. We had less than $15,000 in the bank and some furniture. We had no other assets. The study we were doing belonged to companies we were working for. They said, "Close the business we are calling your note. Send us whatever money you can. We will go after Craig for the rest." We tried to explain that we thought we could be profitable. They didn't care. They understood suing Craig. The investors lost all their equity.

The next day we start closing the company. We collected all the account receivables, paid all the payables, and sent the FDIC less than $20,000. I heard a rich man say "if you never lost any money, you will never make any money." Under that theory I was half way on the road to my success. But it didn't feel that way.

Chuck, Kirby, and I started a new company called Advanced Ergonomics, Inc. We maxed out our bank accounts and credit cards to come up with $15,000. Jim and Ben loaned us $25,000. We finished the study. Chuck was right; it worked. We went to the companies that funded the study and presented a way for us to buy the rights of the research. This became the cornerstone of our business. The three of us would not be paid for months, but it did become profitable.

We had big dreams when we started. But a little dream achieved can be a good thing.

As for Craig, well, he hung on until 1992. He took bankruptcy reorganized, and the paper reports today he worth over a billion dollars. He has all kinds of successful investments. The traits that Jim McCormick admired in Craig served him well. Two other traits did too, his honesty and his firm two handed grip on the throat of tenacity. Craig owns a couple of wineries and I thought it would be pretty cool to buy some of his wine. So I got on their web site and looked around. But after looking at the pricing, I had to pass. Craig is real proud of that wine. Good for him.

As for me, I sold my share to Chuck and Kirby. Kirby calls every month now and tells how much better they are doing now that I am gone. That's not surprising. But, I got to go out on my terms. I can not ask for more than that.

ZOE'S CAREER PATH

Since these are my memoirs, this part will be brief. If she wants them any longer, she can write her own dang memoirs. I know her first job was as a pickup girl. It's not what you think. She worked at a bank. The pickup girls would pick up all the checks and deposits from the cashiers and take them to the back room and make sure everything balanced. She was good at balancing. She is good at spelling, too, so she becomes a secretary for the vice president of the bank.

In the next several years she would become a bank vice president herself. It is not extraordinary today for women to be in high management positions. But when she started working, it was. While she was a secretary, the bank offered people the chance to take an aptitude test to see if they had the ability to learn how to program these new machines called computers. Turns out she does. This would give her a whole new life and career.

I already told you she worked for Honeywell when I first met her. When she gets to Dallas, she goes to work for Affiliated Computers. This is not the same company that exists today. Mercantile National Bank acquired the original company. She had the good sense to leave and go down the street to the First National Bank. She stayed there the rest of her working life. Well, sorta. The First National would become Interfirst, and then First Republic, and then NCNB, and then NationsBank, and then Bank of America. Her ability to program computers leads to her ability to manage project teams for change. As you can tell from the name changes, she has had a lot of opportunity to manage.

She would manage projects all over the world. She worked on projects in Dallas, San Antonio, Abilene, Midland/Odessa, Korea, London, Germany, San Francisco, Portland, Seattle, Charlotte, Boston, Baltimore, and probably others I don't remember, and she did become a

Vice President, not bad for a little girl from Beaumont. She would retire before me and she had more money. This is what you call marrying up!

FEMME FATALE

Every story needs a femme fatale. Leslie would play that role. I was twenty-four, recently married, recently promoted, and recently moved to Dallas. My wife came for a couple of weeks, but returned to Waco to live with her parents. I could have met Leslie in West Texas; she was two years younger and grew up in Odessa, only twenty miles away. Or maybe when I was in law school, she was a student at UT. But I didn't. I met her in Dallas. She had just graduated from college and she was a twenty-two year old hottie.

Our office in Dallas had about fifteen employees. So it was small and everybody pretty much knew everybody's business. It was well known that my wife did not live with me. What was not known until now is what happened next.

Leslie worked in the same office, but her boss was in Austin, mine was in Dallas. One Saturday while I was working, she came by the office for something and invited me to her apartment for a spaghetti dinner. This was the one thing she could cook. I said yes. Now here is where the femme fatale part comes in. After dinner it started with a back rub. I don't remember whose back got rubbed first. A little while later she says "Are you going to do anything or not?" This was a life-changing question.

The next morning, from my apartment, I called my soon- to-be ex wife and informed her of her new status. She said "You called me before breakfast to tell me that?" I wish I had had a snappy answer, but I didn't. The next week her mother and daddy brought their pickup and went through the apartment and took everything that resembled value. They could have brought a Volkswagen.

The legal system would slowly dissolve the marriage. The affair with Leslie would be our secret. Now a classic femme fatale is a beautiful evil woman. Leslie was not evil. But she had a magic spell over me. My hands were always on her. She made no objection. What she made was suggestion. It turns out her previous boyfriend in college was married. By the time the divorce was final, she was no longer interested in me. I would move to Houston and meet Doris Day.

From the time I was twenty-two until I was twenty-eight my romantic history varied. I tried to love a woman who thought of me as a brother, a job I was not applying for. I married a woman I did not love, but it didn't matter because she wouldn't live with me. I found a girl who wanted me, but only if I was married to someone else. Finally, I found someone I loved and wanted to be married to, but she turned me down. It is really a good thing she changed her mind because the next thirty plus years would have been … you fill in the blank.

Two more things I should tell about Leslie. I have not seen her in years, but we do sometimes get Christmas cards from her. She ended up married to a successful businessman. She has three daughters in college. Last I heard she lives very happily in Colorado. I am pleased for her.

The last thing about her is a little strange. About fifteen years ago I have a very vivid dream. I am a GI in France after the Normandy Invasion. Along with some others, I am trapped behind enemy lines. Leslie appears as a young member of the French Underground. She is trying to lead us to safety. I recognize her and know of our connection. I know she does too. But the Germans catch us and kill all of us. The dream ends.

I have wondered was this just some silly dream? Did the cat suck on my hair? Or was this a glimpse at some past life? If so, would there be others? Will I meet her again in the future? Will she again ask me a life-changing question? How will I answer it? Well, it depends. Have I found Zoe?

CHRISTINE

My mother was born in 1922 and married my father when she was eighteen. She told me their first date started with stealing watermelons and ended with a farmer chasing them with a shotgun. For the first sixteen years of my life she was a stay at home mom.

When she turned forty, she wanted to go back to work. It was difficult for her to find a job because businesses were reluctant to hire someone who had been out of the work force so long. I noted this. She did get a job as a secretary for the Boy Scouts of Midland. She held that job for five years and then served as the secretary for the County Extension Agent in Midland for twenty years. She was a really good secretary from what I heard. She could spell. Too bad it was not genetic.

In my business life I would always hire older women to be my secretary. It was okay with me if they were just returning to the work force. Some psycho-babbler might suggest I was hiring my mother. Even if that was so, it was a good decision.

When my father died, I asked my mother a really hard question. "Can you take care of money?" She said, "Yes." And she did.

The last couple years of her life she lived in an assisted living center. Her health was up and down. We decided we needed a power of attorney in case my brother or I had to handle any legal matters for her. So I have my friend John an attorney draw up the papers. He asks me what her full legal name is. I tell him Christine Frances Broxson. When she receives the papers, she calls me and asks "Who is Frances?" I say, "You are." She says "Nope, I am Faye." I guess I don't know my mother as well as I thought.

She was very good at making things. Among the things she made were crochet afghans. She made a lot. I have several. I told her that after she died I was going to give one to my brother each year at Christmas and tell him his mother made it. Her favorite color was pink. Last Christmas Michael got the most God-awful pink afghan you ever saw. But his mother made it. I know she is laughing about that. I also know she was pleased that I sent the Baptist Church $1000 in her memory at Christmas. And I can hear her voice saying, "You mean they didn't even send you a Howdy Dowdy?"

In the early summer of 2004 Jack Fryar and his son-in-law are driving in the hill country of Texas. Outside of San Antonio a tire blows on the RV they were in. The RV rolls over a few times. Luckily, Jack's son-in-law is ok, but Jack dies a couple days later in a San Antonio hospital. I go out to Midland for the funeral. I visit Mother at her apartment. The evening before the service there is a custom called "visitation" at the funeral home. My brother and I are going to attend. We ask mother "Now who exactly are we visiting; the family or the deceased?" She laughs at us and says the family. She was still educating us.

The next day the funeral at the First Baptist Church was almost full, maybe 900 people. My brother asks Maridell, "What would Jack think of this?" She says "He would say they were all here for me." Clearly they were there for both of them. If a funeral can be liberating, his was. Jack's daughter did a marvelous job. I just wished I knew about standing ovations then. As I left Midland that day I was driving my car (a new Corvette) and thinking I am sorry he has died. But I am really glad I knew him. The interstate highway between Midland and Stanton is nineteen miles. I got there in just under 10 minutes. For the rest of the 300 miles I put it on cruise control at 70, and reflected on all the wonderful people I have known in West Texas.

CAROL

Carol is Zoe's younger sister, the fourth and last child of Charlie and Annie. I never visited their house on Avenue E in Beaumont, but I have a vision of a small place cluttered with papers, magazines, and debris stacked high with little paths winding around the mess. I have been told there were poorer people in town, but just barely. So when you think about what the four kids accomplished, it gives high definition to the term humble roots. Charles became a Captain in the Merchant Marines, Bill an executive with IBM, Zoe a vice president with the country's largest bank.

Along the way of life Carol got a degree in English, a Masters in Education, a couple of husbands, and a pretty cool daughter. Now some might say if you didn't know about her education, your first impression might be she fell off the proverbial turnip truck. In truth I am probably the only one to say that. The first time I met her was in California where she and her second husband, Randy, lived with Ellen, her daughter from the first marriage. Are you still with me?

Zoe and I had driven out there on vacation. We got to their house about 4 PM. Carol said the plan was to grill some steaks when Randy got home from work about 6. So we have some cocktails and wine. Now Randy and Carol don't drink much. He gets home on time and gets engrossed in some puzzle that Zoe had brought him. Carol is engrossed in talking. I am engrossed in "When is dinner?" About 9 o' clock I say, "Where is the grill, I will start the fire." At 10 PM I take the steaks off the grill and Zoe serves the salad and other stuff she has prepared. If we had not showed up for the visit, I don't know what they would have eaten. Apparently this was not unusual. Carol likes to say "For dinner I makes reservations!"

Carol was a teacher for a while, but then she became a successful business woman. She was the first person I ever heard of who tutored high school students so they could make higher scores on the SAT test. She is from all accounts very good at this and in northern California she is in high demand. You may have to be on a waiting list to get in her class. So apply now.

Carol and Randy were married in 1972, divorced in 1992. I always admired Randy because Carol's first husband was bad on making child support payments for their daughter. Ellen was seven when Randy married Carol. One time Carol's ex sent only half of the child support amount. Randy sent it back, with a note saying, "We don't take partial payments." Then Randy simply took the attitude, "To hell with him, I don't need his money." So it was not surprising, even after Carol and Randy divorced, that when Ellen was married, Randy walked the bride down the aisle. Carol and Randy have remained friends. Randy is remarried to Nancy, and all of three them get together and Randy cooks or Carol make dinner reservations.

I know I told you about Carl and Jaynne's tattoos. I could tell you about Ellen's. But Carol would really be upset with me if I did. I hope you understand.

The last thing about Carol is this. She is the final proofreader of this work. I have fully disclosed to you, dear reader, that I lack proficiency in this task. I have two software programs to help me. But Carol corrects something on almost every page. Her sense of humor comes through too. For example, in the story about Lou Ann and Bob, I didn't capitalize his name. Carol suggested maybe I meant to belittle him. I wish I was that clever. So if the spelling is wrong or the grammar or typos bother you, you will have to take it up with Carol. Be prepared to cook your own dinner.

RETIREMENT

Zoe retired first and got busy doing some things she always wanted to do. The first was to take the Master Gardeners Course. This is an eight hour per day class that meets once a week for about six months. Everybody had to pass tests, and do seventy hours of volunteer work. She has loved it. Her project so far has taught her how to attract more butterflies to the back yard. She tells me now she is going to be on the board of directors. I am wondering if this will be more about politics than growing things. We will see.

Kirby tells me Jodi wants to retire and raise goats. She wants to make cheese. This Master Gardening thing is sounding better.

As for me, first thing I did after retiring was write this book, and force it on my friends and family. Next, I will try to force it on the rest of the world. But the odds of actually getting it published are about a zillion to one so don't hold your breath. I will take some pride in this work, because Maridell Fryar has seen some early drafts. She told me she had read it three times and had a strong emotional reaction to it. The last time she read any of my work, I was eighteen. She read it once. She had a strong reaction too. She wrote C—needs work.

Retirement and Netflix did bring a new tradition to our house. Sometime, between 3 and 5 PM, we start happy hour movie. Cheers!

ADVICE

The only way to end this book is the way it started. That is with the truth found in my father's poem on reaching a stage in life where you should be able to offer up pearls of wisdom. As he says nobody cares. That of course will not stop me.

Given my experience with the opposite sex I am uniquely qualified to say, "Find a good one and hang on, but not too tight as that tends to irritate the good ones."

My friend Phil Davis once said that the key to success is hard work. After some thinking about that, he was almost right. It is hard work on the right things. Think about all those corporate crooks that worked hard and ended up in jail. They were hard at work all right but found no success. I think the key is to decide what it is that you want to be successful at, and then work hard, and if you can get other people to work hard on things you want done—then all the better.

One other thing about success is being able to work on your on agenda. When I was fifty-seven I decided I wanted to learn to play the guitar. I worked on it. Eight months after I started I am able to play and sing one of my mother's favorite songs for her, my brother, Jack, and Maridell Fryar. That was the biggest stage I ever played and fear was a strong reality. But I did it anyway. And as bad as it was, it was still very successful.

Life comes at us very fast. We have to react to it. That gets in the way of being able to set your own agenda. I have found that when I can do what I want. I accomplished more. I worked for two very successful Doctors. They would give me about a hundred ideas a week to run to ground. If I ignored the ideas there would be hell to pay. Now in all honesty most of the things they suggested were not all that good. But sometimes there was a gold nugget. The problem was I never knew which one was going to be the nugget. So, I thought I was distracted from my agenda. But since, I worked for them I decided that my agenda would include their suggestions. I consider this good advice.

Practice makes perfect. This is not true. Goofing around at practice is not going to make anything perfect. Perfect practice makes perfect.

That is the end of the soap box. I hope you enjoyed some of it.

978-0-595-42146-6
0-595-42146-6